Apprehensive again, Beth reduced the door's opening to a crack. "Yes?"

He took off his hat, and the raw wind instantly whipped his bronze-blond hair into a tangled strawstack. "You *are* Bethany Curtis?"

He sounded doubtful, and she was tempted to confirm that doubt and send him on his way. Before she could say anything, however, baby Joey woke with a lusty yowl. The man's head jerked up, his gaze probing the room beyond the barrier of her body.

Beth studied him more closely. Fair skin beneath the tan, darker streaks of bronze and chestnut in the deep gold of his hair, thick brows and lashes of the same leonine shades. The silver-gray eyes flicked back to her and, with an electric jolt, she suddenly knew why he looked so familiar. Why the baby's cry interested him. Why he was here.

Palisades.
Pure Romance.

Fiction that features credible characters and entertaining plot lines, while continuing to uphold strong Christian values. From high adventure to tender stories of the heart, each Palisades Romance is an undiluted story of love, from beginning to end!

ESCAPE

LORENA McCOURTNEY

PALISADES

ESCAPE
published by Palisades
a part of the Questar publishing family

© 1996 by Lorena McCourtney
International Standard Book Number:1-57673-012-3

Cover illustration by George Angelini
Cover designed by David Carlson and
Mona Weir-Daly
Edited by Diane Noble

Printed in the United States of America

For information:
QUESTAR PUBLISHERS, INC.
POST OFFICE BOX 1720
SISTERS, OREGON 97759

96 97 98 99 00 01 02 03 — 10 9 8 7 6 5 4 3 2 1

*With special thanks to my Aunt Phoebe
and my stepdaughter Sherrie,
for their enthusiastic support of my books.*

❧

*While I live will I praise the LORD;
I will sing praises unto my God while I have any being.*

PSALM 146:2, KJV

One

❧

Ryman Springs, Oklahoma
January, 1933

I f Beth hadn't been standing on a chair, trying to wedge a rag into a crack above the warped old window frame, she'd never have seen the sleek automobile pull into the yard. Nor would she have heard the smooth purr of the engine over the howl of the Oklahoma wind whipping a bitter blend of dust and snow across the bare ground…or over the rattle and slam of her old roof's rusty metal patches lifting precariously in the powerful gusts.

She pushed the dangling strip of blue rag aside and stared in astonishment at the long, racy silver car that exuded expensive elegance in spite of a rude speckling of road dust and mud. Just as astonishing was the man who stepped out of the car, his hands busy keeping the wind from tearing the stylish, snap-brim hat from his head and the car door from its hinges.

He leaned into the wind, one hand still on the hat, as he headed for her front door. Instead of the rugged work clothes common to most of the local farmers and ranchers, he wore a long, fawn-colored overcoat and dark slacks with a neat cuff.

He must be lost, she decided. He was probably looking for directions to another town. Or maybe he was some big-city banker trying to locate a bankrupt farm his institution was repossessing. In which case he wouldn't get any help from *her,* she thought with a spirited sense of loyalty toward the hardworking families whose children she had taught the past two and a half years.

He glanced up just before reaching the rickety wooden steps. He looked momentarily startled when his eyes met Beth's gazing down at him from her unlikely position near the top of the window. Beth had never seen him before, of that she was certain. He was in his late twenties, long-legged, tall, his shoulders a rugged framework under the expensive coat. There was an aura of urban sophistication and boardroom self-confidence about him, but his angular features bore the contrast of a sunburned tan as deep as that of any local cowboy.

No, she'd never seen him before, and he was too good-looking to be easily forgotten. Yet there was an odd familiarity about the silver-gray eyes and aristocratic slant of cheekbones. A familiarity that unexpectedly sent warning fingers of apprehension crawling up her spine.

This is ridiculous, she chided herself, briskly climbing down from the chair.

Yet when his knock rattled the door another wave of that peculiar uneasiness jolted her. Except for baby Joey napping in the bedroom, she was alone here. She had no telephone, and her small teacher's cottage was tucked off by itself behind the brick schoolhouse, with only the windswept prairie beyond. If he was seeking directions, why had he bypassed the hotel and train station and other houses and come here?

When the door didn't instantly open, he knocked again, harder, obviously not a man long on patience. "I'm looking for Miss Bethany Curtis," he called. "Are you in there, Miss Curtis?"

Now the chill that crept up her spine wasn't from the cold

air seeping through the drafty old cottage. How did he know her name?

The answer embarrassed her. He'd no doubt come in response to one of the many job applications she had sent out. And here she was, hiding like a scared rabbit! She was, thank the Lord, no longer in desperate need of a job, but she certainly owed a courteous reception to someone who had taken the time and effort to come in person to see her.

She opened the door a crack, but a blast of cold wind, besides whipping her auburn hair in a stormy froth, nearly wrenched it from her hands. About the time she raised her eyes to meet her visitor, she was struck by how unlikely it was that she would receive an in-person response to any of those applications. In these disastrous depression times of 1933, with dozens of applicants for every job, no out-of-town school board member was going to rush to her home with an eager job offer.

Apprehensive again, she reduced the door's opening to a crack. "Yes?"

He took off his hat, and the raw wind instantly whipped his bronze-blond hair into a tangled strawstack. "You *are* Bethany Curtis?"

He sounded doubtful, and she was tempted to confirm that doubt and send him on his way. Before she could say anything, however, baby Joey woke with a lusty yowl. The man's head jerked up, his gaze probing the room beyond the barrier of her body.

Beth studied him more closely. Fair skin beneath the tan, darker streaks of bronze and chestnut in the deep gold of his hair, thick brows and lashes of the same leonine shades. The silver-gray eyes flicked back to her and, with an electric jolt, she suddenly knew why he looked so familiar. Why the baby's cry interested him. Why he was here.

A steel fist knotted in her stomach. At first, she had expected just such a visit, but as the months passed her fears had shrunk to an occasional nervous qualm. Now fear returned like a breath-crushing band around her chest.

She swallowed. She must not be afraid. She had *right* on her side. *"I think they'll want him,"* her sister-in-law Sylvia had written her months ago, as if she had some inner knowledge that her baby would be a boy. *"I think they'll make a determined effort to get him. But don't let them, Beth. Money is my father's god, and possessions are his temple, and I don't want my baby trapped in that world. If your brother and I aren't here to raise our baby ourselves, we want you to do it, Beth. You. I love my family, but I don't want my baby raised to become like them."*

"What do you want?" Beth asked. As if she didn't know.

"May I come inside where we can carry on a conversation without shouting over the wind?"

"Who are you?" The real question, of course, was which *one* of them was he?

"I'm Guy Wilkerson, Sylvia's brother."

Guy. The younger of Sylvia's two older brothers. The one who had attended Harvard. The one who drove race cars. The one who carried out his father's iron-fisted orders.

"What do you want?" she repeated.

"I really must talk to you."

Reluctantly, aware he wasn't going away until they did talk, Beth opened the door to let him in. Inside, out of the raw wind, he smoothed his disheveled hair with a hand that looked surprisingly rough and weathered against the pristine white cuff of his shirt. His alert gaze flicked around Beth's meager home, taking in the leak stains on the ceiling, the smelly old stove that hiccuped puffs of smoke as wind gusted down the chimney, and the ragged diapers drying on a makeshift clothesline strung behind the stove. His roving eyes paused only on the unfinished painting of Joey on her easel. In spite of her hostility toward him she felt embarrassed having him see her amateurish artwork. She'd done paintings of many of her students, to the awed delight of parents and relatives, but in the wealthy setting to which Guy Wilkerson belonged, he no doubt lived with fine art, *real* art, every day.

He tilted his head at the painting. "Joseph?"

Joseph. Her mind blanked for a moment. She never thought of Joey as "Joseph," but that was his name, of course. Joseph Albert Curtis.

"Yes," she said warily.

He turned back to her without comment on the painting. "You're not an easy person to find."

Under his appraising gaze, Beth was uncomfortably aware of the old brown skirt, shapeless cardigan sweater and heavy stockings she wore as defense against the house's cold drafts. She resisted an urge to tug at the sagging stockings or gather her windblown hair into some semblance of order.

"I didn't know you were looking." Beth clenched her fists lightly to keep her hands from fidgeting nervously.

"We made inquiries about the child after Sylvia's death. Surely you must have realized that when the father was killed and the baby became an orphan, that we'd want to know."

Yes, she'd known. After the "inquiries" the Wilkersons made through a lawyer after Sylvia's death, inquiries that disparaged Mark's capabilities as a father, along with what almost amounted to an offer to *buy* the baby? Of course she'd known.

"But instead of notifying us you simply snatched the child and disappeared. We as Joseph's family—"

Beth lifted her head defiantly. "I am also—" She paused and then also used Guy's formal terminology. "—Joseph's family. I did not 'snatch' him, nor did I 'disappear.' I simply brought him home with me."

"But you didn't notify us of Sylvia's husband's death," he repeated. His tone said more, that this wasn't simply a dereliction of duty but a deliberate deception.

"The Wilkerson family hated and scorned my brother while he was alive." Beth didn't even try to keep the contempt from her own voice. Mark, loving, caring, generous Mark, and the Wilkersons had treated him as if he were some wild-eyed fanatic out to worm his way into the family fortunes! "I saw no reason to think you'd care any more about him in death. None of you even bothered to attend Sylvia's funeral."

A shadow of something…sorrow? regret? guilt?…briefly crossed Guy's angular features. "It wasn't necessarily a lack of interest or caring. Sylvia had unfortunately chosen to disassociate herself from the family."

"Disassociate!" Beth repeated, outraged by the word. "The Wilkerson family cut her off! Your father told her if she defied him and married my brother that he wanted nothing more to do with her!"

"Whatever the situation, it's all in the past," Guy countered smoothly. Just as smoothly he abandoned accusation and shifted to a new tactic. "It's unfair, of course, that you should have the burden of raising their child—"

"He's no burden!" Beth returned hotly. "I love him."

This time Guy pointedly let his gaze flow from the threadbare carpet to the faded, cabbage-rose wallpaper and blue rag still dangling at the window. She'd done what she could to brighten the dark rooms, draping the windows with ruffled yellow curtains, making colorful pillows for the old horsehair sofa and putting up several of her unframed paintings, but nothing could change the general dreariness. Eventually his gaze returned to Beth.

She simply stared back at him defiantly. Neither her shabby home nor clothes were important. Joey was. And he had never gone hungry, never gone without clean clothes or bath or love or attention.

Joey howled again. "If you'll excuse me…" Beth murmured.

She hurried to the bedroom and changed Joey's diaper. He gurgled and kicked, lifting his arms to be carried to the other room for their usual playtime. At seven months he could already crawl like a small whirlwind, and he loved to be read or sung to, or play a little game of Beth choo-chooing and churning his plump legs like a locomotive.

"Later," Beth whispered, leaning over the crib to give him a kiss on his sweet little tummy. "You play with your rattle and be quiet as a little mouse for just a few minutes."

She jumped as something brushed her shoulder and she found Guy Wilkerson standing by the crib with her. She should have closed the door. Although that wouldn't necessarily have kept him out, she decided uneasily, as she watched him put a rough finger against Joey's tiny palm.

"He shows his Wilkerson blood."

At this age, Joey's wispy hair was pale baby blond rather than Guy's darker bronze-gold, but his coloring and something about his forehead indeed revealed his Wilkerson family connections. But his eyes already blazed the intense Curtis blue that Beth and her brother had shared. And there was perhaps a bit of the stubborn Curtis chin as well.

Joey's fist latched on to Guy's finger, and the sudden tenderness in Guy's smile surprised Beth. As did the softness and hint of awe in his voice when he said, "He's really a husky little fellow, isn't he?" He paused and swallowed. "I can see Sylvia in him."

Unexpectedly, Beth had the impression that wasn't necessarily the same as seeing the "Wilkerson blood."

"He's sitting up and crawling now," she said warily. "And he has two teeth."

Joey obligingly showed off the teeth in a big, drooling grin.

"May I hold him?"

Beth's first instinct was, *No! Stay away from my baby!*

"I'm not going to grab him and run," Guy said gently.

He took off the overcoat and draped it over the foot of the crib. Reluctantly, Beth picked up the baby and set him upright in Guy's arms. Joey studied this strange new person with wide-eyed curiosity.

"Do you have children, Mr. Wilkerson?" Beth asked the question, even though the cautious, inexperienced way he handled the baby was enough to tell her this was a rare, if not unique experience for him.

"No, I'm not married."

Grudgingly she gave Guy credit for effort as he didn't even flinch when Joey planted a hand on his face and commenced an undignified exploration. Not many bachelors, Beth suspected, would appreciate such a thorough nose probing by baby fingers. Nor the accompanying dribble of baby drool on the immaculate white shirt front.

But Guy just laughed, and so did Beth. There was something magical about a big man and a small baby together.

"Do I pass inspection?" Guy asked, cooperatively putting his head down so Joey could grab a lock of dark gold hair. Joey grabbed the hair, suddenly took a long look at the unfamiliar face beneath it and screwed his own face into a mask of tears.

"Maybe not," Guy added ruefully as he returned the howling baby to Beth's outstretched arms.

Joey instantly stopped crying and, from the haven of safety snuggled against Beth's breast, peeked mischievously at Guy.

"Did I do something wrong?" Guy asked, his bewilderment

lending an unexpected touch of boyish appeal to his masculine features.

"No. Babies are like that. Instant changes of mood. Smiles to tears and back again, all in the space of a few eye blinks."

Beth put Joey back in his crib and gave him his favorite rattle. She also handed Guy his coat and walked to the door as if she expected him to follow. For a moment they had shared a small, unexpected bond in their feelings for this baby who was nephew to them both. But in truth, they were bitter adversaries, and they may as well get down to drawing the battle lines.

Guy, with one last look at the baby, did follow. Beth snapped the door shut, feeling safer with that barrier between Guy and Joey.

"You appear to have done a fine job of caring for him," Guy said. As if he intended to stay awhile, he draped his coat over one of the chairs flanking the round oak table. "I understand you're a teacher, Miss Curtis?"

"Yes." Beth did not invite him to sit. She did not intend for him to stay.

"And this house is provided for you by the school?"

"Yes." She flexed her hands nervously. What was he getting at?

"But I see no children around the schoolhouse, and you're not in the classroom. I understand that the school is, in fact, closed."

She edged to her right, putting the old oak table between them and pressing her fingertips against the scarred surface. "Many families have left the area because of the difficult economic conditions. With reduced attendance and a lack of funds, the school board decided at Thanksgiving to close the school for the remainder of the year."

"Which means you have been without employment for

17

almost two months." His gaze went to her purse lying on the table as if he could see through the faded blue cloth to the coins inside. "A new teaching position will not be easy to find in the middle of the school year. And how about your living quarters? Undoubtedly they will not be available indefinitely."

So that was it. He was suggesting she and Joey were soon going to be dumped homeless on the street. It was with no attempt to conceal a certain triumph that she smiled and refuted that implication.

"But I *have* secured other employment." She would not have been able to make that statement a week earlier. After sending out dozens of inquiries and applications, all of which were ignored or rejected, a job offer had finally come through, and she was now only waiting for instructions on when to report for work.

"I see." His tanned brow wrinkled in a small, displeased frown. "You'll be working here in Ryman Springs?"

"No. I'll be teaching fourth- and fifth-graders in Oklahoma City. The regular teacher became ill and can't finish out the year."

"How can you manage to teach and care for a baby at the same time?" he asked skeptically, efficiently marshaling a new line of attack on her ability to care for Joey properly.

"He's always stayed in the classroom with me here."

"That may not be possible in a different school."

That was true, and it was a problem that concerned Beth. But she could surely find some caring young mother who would be glad to earn a little extra money by adding Joey to her household during the day. Someday Beth hoped to make a full-time living with her artwork, which would enable her to work at home, but that dream, she knew, was not likely to come true soon in these harsh economic times.

"Miss Curtis, let's stop dancing around the real issue here and get down to business." Guy's tone turned hard and decisive. "Joseph is important to our family. There are no other grandchildren. My brother Warren and his wife are childless, and, as I mentioned earlier, I'm not even married. And my father has a strong interest in preserving the continuity of the family bloodline."

Beth could almost laugh at this pompous reference to "family bloodline," as if the Wilkersons possessed some rare noble lineage that must be nourished and immortalized. Nat Wilkerson, Beth knew from what Sylvia had said, had started out as a rough-and-tough wildcatter in the Texas oil fields and clawed his way up the financial and social ladders to wealth and status. Beth doubted she knew the full extent of the Wilkerson family's diversified holdings, but, growing up in St. Louis, she was familiar with the Wilkerson textile factory there. From Sylvia, she'd also heard of banking interests, a stockyard and meat-packing plant in Iowa, and a resort hotel in Florida. And much of that wealth, Sylvia had suspected, although she'd been kept far removed from any unpleasant details, had been acquired without concern for ethics or moral responsibility.

Yet Beth couldn't laugh, after all, because the Wilkerson's power and ruthless determination threw a dangerous shadow over anything in their path. Which was exactly where she stood, between them and Joey. Her fingertips crushed deeper into the oak table, as if grain of wood and whorl of fingerprints were becoming one.

"That's why you have come, then. Because you want Joseph."

"Yes."

The battle lines were drawn. Joey was no small bond between them now. He *was* the battle line.

Guy reached into an inner pocket of the fawn-colored coat. "I have here a legal document for your signature—"

She didn't touch the folded papers he extended to her. "A document that says what?"

"That you are turning full custody of Joseph over to us."

Curiosity, not a weakening of determination concerning Joey, made Beth ask, "And if I should sign this document, what happens then? You're going to load a seven-months-old baby into your car and take care of him while driving back to St. Louis?"

"We'll send a driver and nanny for him in a few days."

"And then what?"

"He becomes a member of the family. He'll live in the family mansion in St. Louis, with the best of everything. Servants, travel, culture, the finest education, every advantage available."

"Being taken care of by nannies and governesses."

Guy looked suddenly wary, as if he suspected a trap. "My brother's wife Carolyn will no doubt have a motherly hand in his upbringing. And you may rest assured that any nanny or governess who cares for him will be most capable."

Beth assumed she was supposed to be dazzled. She was not.

"Sylvia had all that, and she said she was never truly happy, never really knew what life and love were all about, until she found the Lord and married my brother." And love, Beth noted, was not among the list of benefits on Guy's list.

Beth expected indignation or hostile argument, but unexpectedly Guy merely smiled and shrugged. "Ah, yes. Love and religion. A powerful, if occasionally misguided, combination. I suppose, because your brother was a minister, you share his religious convictions."

"Mark and I were raised by our grandparents, who were lifelong Christians, and I asked Jesus to come into my life many years ago." Which was how Mark and Sylvia had wanted their son raised, and how he would *not* be raised if he were with the Wilkersons. Nat Wilkerson, Sylvia's father, had been as set against her taking up "religion" as he was against her marrying Mark Curtis. "Sylvia said that when you were a child you also gave your heart to the Lord."

Guy looked momentarily disconcerted at having this bit of his past flung at him. He made a disparaging gesture with one hand.

"Yes, I did. I think I was...what? Perhaps twelve or thirteen. Not exactly of an age to make major life decisions." He smiled as if they were reminiscing about some lovable but foolish childhood prank. "About that same age I loved adventure books, and once decided that when I grew up I'd take off for the jungle and become another Tarzan."

"Adventure books and the Bible are hardly comparable—"

Guy smoothly cut her off. "Well, we got off on a rather irrelevant sidetrack there, didn't we? Now, back to Joseph."

"Joseph," Beth said flatly, "is staying with me."

Guy went on as if she hadn't even spoken. "We'll reimburse you for any expenses you may have incurred in his care." Apparently noting the blue flash of scorn in her eyes he added, "In fact, I'm sure we can also add a generous salary for your excellent care of him these past months."

"Mr. Wilkerson," Beth cut in with raw hostility, *"My nephew is not for sale."*

"Of course not!" he agreed heartily. He smiled. "Although, if enough money is involved, almost anything is for sale." His silver-gray eyes flicked over her as if he were casually evaluating her price.

"The Wilkerson family motto, I take it? *If enough money is offered, anything is for sale.*"

His head jerked, as if he were momentarily taken aback by the hostile taunt. Then as smoothly as a ballroom dancer, he glided in a different direction. "Obviously you care a great deal for Joseph, so it must also be obvious to you that we have much more to offer him than you do."

Beth picked up his coat and hat and handed them to him. She walked to the door and put a hand on the knob. "I'm sorry you wasted your time making this trip, Mr. Wilkerson. But you may inform your father that his grandson is healthy, happy, and in good hands."

Guy tapped the hat against his leg. Narrow frown lines appeared on his forehead. "Miss Curtis, I've tried to be diplomatic, but this is not just a request. We *will* have Joseph. He belongs with us."

Beth swallowed, desperately trying to hammer down the fear that determined statement aroused in her. In a legal battle, she could never defeat the Wilkerson's money and power. But she resolutely gave no sign of that inner panic when she said, "I have a letter from Sylvia specifically stating her desire that if this circumstance ever arose, I was to raise their child. It also specifically stated that she did *not* want anyone from her side of the family to have him. I believe that would have considerable weight in any legal confrontation."

Beth knew the fact that she had such a letter came as an unpleasant surprise to Guy, although his controlled reaction was no more than a metallic flare of gray eyes and a sharp swallow.

"It doesn't matter what the letter says. It is not a binding legal document. Can you even prove its authenticity? And no court on earth is going to consign a child to this—" A scornful flick of his gaze encompassed everything from the humble house to Beth's unfashionable clothing. "—when he could have all we have to offer."

"Money and mansions aren't everything. A judge may take that into consideration."

"There is more than one judge in this world, Miss Curtis, and more than one court of law in which to seek a decision." He smiled lightly. "And I rather imagine our funds will hold out longer than yours."

The threat was plain. If one judge decided against them, they would simply find another judge. And they definitely could afford to keep that up longer than she could.

Beth shivered with apprehension, but she simply turned the doorknob and let in a crack of cold air.

"This is your final decision, then?" Guy asked. "You refuse to turn Joseph over to us?"

"This is my final decision."

He tried once more, apparently unable to comprehend that the weapon which usually served the Wilkersons so well was not working here. "We're willing to compensate you very generously, Miss Curtis. Surely a woman as lovely as you has ambitions beyond—" He glanced out the window, where only a single winter-bare skeleton of a tree held back the endless prairie. "—beyond this dreary existence."

"As I told you, I'll be leaving soon to accept another position."

"Where you'll still be trapped with the burden of raising a child alone, with inadequate resources."

Beth flung the door open wide, ignoring the harsh spit of snow in her face and the fierce wind that tangled her hair and molded her sweater and skirt against her body. "Get out, Mr. Wilkerson."

"You'll regret this." He flung the coat around his shoulders, jammed the hat on his head and raked her with steel eyes as he stalked to the door. "This isn't the end of the matter, you know."

She slammed the door so hard that he had to jump to keep from getting his heels caught in it. The lock on the door was broken, but she grabbed a straight-backed chair and braced it under the knob. She rushed to the window, feeling a certain satisfaction when the wind snatched his hat and sailed it across the prairie like some expensive tumbleweed.

Guy was halfway to the car when something else sailed across the yard. Beth recognized it instantly as the flat, rusty piece of metal old Silas Downs had used to patch her leaky roof. The wind had whipped it loose, and with deadly accuracy it now swooped like some malevolent metal bird directly at Guy Wilkerson.

"Watch out!" Beth screamed.

The rusty square of metal slammed into the back of Guy's head. He staggered and collapsed on his hands and knees. Beth yanked the door open and ran to him. Blood streamed from the gash, a garish crimson flood against his blond hair. The raw wind knifed through her clothing and windblown snow stung her face, but she managed to drape his left arm around her shoulders, wrap her right arm around his waist, and lever him to his feet.

"What happened?" he mumbled.

"You got hit with a piece of metal that blew off the roof."

He wobbled to one side, and it took all Beth's strength to keep them both from crashing to the ground as she helped him across the yard.

"We're at the steps now. Lift your foot."

Like an obedient child he raised the foot to an exaggerated height and set it down carefully.

"Now the other one." He repeated the motion. Warm speckles of blood mixed with icy flakes of blowing snow hit Beth's face.

Inside, she helped him to the old horsehair sofa. He sat with his elbows on his knees, dazed, head bowed between his hands. Blood trickled through his fingers.

She raced to the linen shelf in her bedroom. She had exactly one extra set of flannel sheets for her bed, but she ripped a strip from the end of a sheet and folded it into a heavy pad. She returned to the living room and pressed the pad against the gash, using her other hand on his forehead to steady him.

"What are you doing?"

"I'm trying to stop the bleeding. Pressure on a wound will help do that."

"How badly am I hurt?"

"I can't tell. The blow didn't knock you unconscious, but you may need stitches." She moved Guy's hand up to the pad that was already seeping blood. "Here. Hold that against your head. *Tight.*"

"What are you going to do?" He sounded apprehensive, as if he thought she might be planning to whip out needle and thread and start stitching him up on the spot.

"I'm taking you to Dr. Atkins over in Warden."

Guy had enough spirit left to mutter, "I'm not going to let some incompetent backwoods horse doctor start sewing on my head!"

Dr. Atkins was neither incompetent nor a "backwoods horse doctor," although he had been known to stitch up a beloved dog or two, but all Beth said to Guy was, "I'm afraid you haven't much choice."

Beth ran to the bedroom, made another pad for the wound, and wrapped Joey in a heavy blanket. Carrying the child, she got her old green coat and a baby bottle from the kitchen.

"How far is it to the doctor?" Guy asked.

"About thirty miles."

"You have a car?"

"No. We'll take yours."

That was enough to make his head jerk up in spite of his injury. "That's my new Packard! Do you know how to drive?"

"More or less." She felt no obligation to reassure him about her driving abilities. "Although if you'd prefer to walk…"

He settled back on the sofa, muttering something that sounded derogatory even though unintelligible.

At the car, Beth shoved Guy's expensive suede suitcase to the far side of the backseat and got Joey settled, then returned to help Guy across the snow-whipped yard. The Packard's caramel-colored seats had a luxurious, buttery softness and rich scent of new leather, and the snug interior of the car encircled them like a secure haven that neither snow nor wind could penetrate.

"Boyfriend teach you to drive?" Guy inquired as she inspected the gearshift and various knobs and buttons before starting the engine. It seemed an odd question under the circumstances, almost a roundabout way of asking if she had someone special in her life.

"My brother Mark taught me," she replied flatly. She inquired about certain knobs and switches, and Guy, one hand holding the second pad to his head, grudgingly explained their use to her. The engine rumbled to life smoothly, the starter button a big improvement over the crank starter on the old Model-T on which she'd learned to drive. She carefully backed the car in a wide arc. Guy's eyes were closed, although whether in pain from the injury or apprehension about her competence to handle his expensive car, she was uncertain.

She drove with equal care through the small town, although with only two moving cars and a half-dozen parked vehicles on the wide main street, there was little danger of hitting anything. They crossed the railroad tracks and traveled in silence for several miles, the only sounds the powerful purr of the engine and Joey's contented baby noises. It was only midafternoon, but clouds and blowing snow dimmed everything to a murky gray-white. By now blood smeared Guy's face and stained his fawn-colored coat.

"Why are you doing this for me?" His eyes were still closed, and he sounded more resentful than appreciative.

"I couldn't just leave you lying there." Tartly she added, "You were making a very messy puddle of blood in my front yard."

He opened his eyes. "I intruded into your home. I was unpleasant. I threatened you. And still you're helping me."

"We can't limit our help to those of whom we approve."

"I suppose this is all part of some noble, generous Christian duty," he muttered. "Love your enemy, turn the other cheek, and all that do-gooder garbage. Now I'm supposed to see the light and suddenly become a good Christian myself."

"You might find it a rewarding change from intruding and threatening," Beth snapped, at the moment feeling neither generous nor noble toward Guy Wilkerson. She also needed to keep her full attention on the unfamiliar car and a road that was sometimes almost invisible in the swirling snow.

At the big brick house where Dr. Atkins lived and had his medical practice, Mrs. Atkins took one alarmed look at the blood dripping from Guy's head and hurried him directly in to see the doctor. Beth offered Joey his bottle as she waited in the outer room, and he drank most of the milk before drifting into a nap.

She caressed his fine blond hair with her fingertips as a sharp, fresh scent of antiseptic floated out from the other room. Her fingers trembled, and she had to resist an urge to clutch the baby to her fiercely. Could the Wilkersons actually take him from her?

She thought about the day that Sylvia had given her the letter. She had gone to stay with Mark and Sylvia as soon as school was out last summer to help Sylvia in her final weeks of pregnancy. It was a good pregnancy, no problems, so she was shocked when Sylvia gave her the sealed envelope with instructions that it was to be opened only if something happened to both her and Mark. That June day in Arkansas had been delightfully sunny, with a drone of bees and fragrance of yellow roses outside the tiny manse the church provided for their pastor, and the letter lay in Beth's hand like some grim omen.

"Oh, don't look so appalled," Sylvia had said with a laugh and her usual sunny cheerfulness, only an uncharacteristic shadow in her gray eyes betraying some ominous foreboding about the future. "You'll probably never have to open it."

Yet all too soon Beth was ripping that sealed envelope open, hands shaking as tears blurred the words written in Sylvia's elegant, finishing-school handwriting.

The baby had come early, turned the wrong way; the labor was long and punishing, the delivery horrendous. The doctor's valiant efforts had saved Joey, but nothing he did could save Sylvia from the raging infection that followed. They buried her when Joey was only a week old, the church packed by a congregation that had loved this sweet, lovely wife of their pastor.

Beth had stayed on, of course, to help Mark with the new baby. Yet only six weeks later Mark, too, was gone, drowned saving a little boy who swam too far out in the nearby river. Three days later his body lay beside Sylvia's in the hillside cemetery behind the church, Beth stunned and overwhelmed by the double loss. She felt as if her world was whirling wildly out of control, as if it had become a place where old rules didn't apply and anything could happen.

She went often to the Lord, but visions of Mark and Sylvia

clouded her eyes when she tried to read her Bible. One moonlit August night she found herself sitting between the twin graves, baby Joey in her arms, not even remembering how she had gotten there but oddly angry because the night was so beautiful, all silver and shadows and sweet fragrance of new-mown hay from a field just beyond the cemetery fence. Somehow that wasn't fair, with Mark and Sylvia cold in the ground beneath her.

It was the letter, the letter that had first slipped her mind in the midst of so much shock and tragedy, that helped dispel that floundering, helpless feeling that everything was out of control, helped her remember that, although God's workings could not always be understood, he *was* always in control.

Perhaps she should immediately have gone through some legal process, she now acknowledged, but at the time the letter had seemed sufficient barrier against the Wilkersons' greedy tentacles. Now she had the uneasy feeling the letter was no more than a flimsy piece of paper that some clever lawyer could demolish or discredit with a few well-paid words.

Guy returned to the waiting room some forty-five minutes later, a professional-looking bandage encompassing his head like a turban. The blood had been cleaned from his face, but scarlet blotches still stained the white shirt.

"The patient is going to be just fine," Dr. Atkins said cheerfully. "No signs of concussion, and the bleeding has stopped. I had to cut away the hair so I could sew up the wound." He grinned. "I'm not much of a barber."

With the bandage around Guy's head, whatever damage Dr. Atkins may have done to his stylish haircut was not visible. The tan now seemed to ride on the surface of pale skin underneath, and the gray eyes had a silvery glaze, but he seemed reasonably steady on his feet.

"Take a couple of those tablets if you need them for pain, and see your own doctor as soon as you get back to St. Louis," Dr. Atkins instructed. "But don't try to drive anywhere tonight."

Dr. Atkins would conscientiously treat any patient who came to him in need, but Beth knew, from the doctor's friendly attitude, that he had no inkling of Guy's ominous purpose here in Oklahoma. While Guy settled the bill with Mrs. Atkins, the doctor chatted with Beth and checked Joey's ears for any sign of an earlier infection.

Back on the road, they drove in silence. The wind had let up, leaving a couple of inches of snow on the rural road, the pristine white broken only by a single pair of tire tracks. After several miles Guy abruptly took a couple of the white pills from his pocket, gulped them down without water and closed his eyes.

He looked oddly vulnerable sitting there with thick lashes lying against his cheek, a faint bluish tinge to his eyelids, and a stub of chopped-off blond hair sticking out from under the turban-bandage, but Beth rejected anything more than a temporary sympathy for his painful wound. Guy Wilkerson, whatever his situation at the moment, was not a vulnerable man. He was out to take away the most precious part of her life, next to the Lord himself, and she had to figure out what to do to thwart those intentions.

No other cars were moving on the town's wide, unpaved main street when they arrived in Ryman Springs near dark. A dull yellow light glimmered in the train station where old LaMar Miner was probably napping. Only two trains a day came through Ryman Springs, one heading east, one west. The few streetlights glowed gently in the wintry dusk, their shallow pools of light softening the gloomy desolation of abandoned buildings and boarded-up storefronts, victims of the hard times. A lamp on the check-in counter dimly silhouetted the name Ryman Springs Hotel arched in flaking golden letters across a grimy window of the only three-story building in town.

Guy roused as the car slowed, grimaced and grabbed his head to steady it. Beth stopped the car across the street from the hotel, which usually housed only a few old-timers living there at low rates.

"You can get a room here, and I'll walk home."

He glanced across the street at the rundown hotel, which she wryly suspected carried all the appeal of another blow on the head for him, but all he said was, "Carrying the baby? You can't do that."

"The doctor said you shouldn't drive yet."

Guy unexpectedly reached across the seat and brushed a loose tendril of auburn hair from the curve of her cheek. "Are you always so kind and considerate to your enemies?"

"I don't know that I've ever had any enemies." Although the words *until now* came to mind.

"Didn't you, when that chunk of metal hit me, think, 'Good. He deserved that'?"

"I did feel a certain satisfaction when your hat blew away," Beth admitted. "But I couldn't let you lie there bleeding."

"You're missing the opportunity of a lifetime, you know."

"What do you mean?"

"We're a wealthy family, Bethany. My father is a hard man, but he isn't a cheap one. He's willing to pay, and pay well, for what he wants. And he wants his grandson very much. You could squeeze a lot of money out of us."

"Why are you telling me this?"

He lifted one shoulder in a half-shrug. "You did me a favor. I suppose I owe you one." He frowned, then put a hand to his head as if the frown had stretched the skin painfully. "Or maybe squeezing us is what you *are* doing."

"Pretending I won't give up the baby in hopes that you'll offer more money? No, Mr. Wilkerson. I told you, Joseph is not for sale. I don't want your money."

"Without even knowing how much?"

"The amount doesn't matter."

"You'd be smart to take it. Because eventually you're going to lose the baby anyway, and then you won't have him *or* the money."

Beth's palms dampened against the expensive, leather-covered steering wheel, but her answer did not change. "No." She hesitated, wanting to be fair in spite of Guy Wilkerson's stubborn belief that Joey could be bought with money or threats. "But I would be willing to bring him to St. Louis for an occasional visit. Perhaps, when he's older, he could even spend a few weeks there during the summer."

"That wouldn't satisfy my father. Nat wants his grandson where he can exert a full-time influence on his life."

"Raise him up to be another financial tycoon?" Beth glanced back at Joey sleeping peacefully, unaware his future was at stake. "Teach him to play with piles of silver dollars rather than wooden blocks? Ride the stock market instead of a bicycle?"

"There's nothing wrong with learning how to make money! Bethany—" he began.

No one who knew her called her that, but she didn't tell him. The switch from Miss Curtis to Bethany was, in fact, a greater intimacy than she wanted from Guy Wilkerson, and she certainly didn't want him calling her Beth.

"Bethany, you're a generous, caring, responsible person. I'm sure you want what's best for Joseph. Doesn't it occur to you that *we* are the ones who can do the most for him, that you are being unfair and selfish in wanting to keep him?"

The possibility of her own selfishness was a jolting thought for Beth, because she fervently did want to keep Joey with her. She wanted to be with him when he said his first word, took his first step, said his first prayer. But after a long minute of serious soul-searching she could truthfully say, "If I truly believed Joey would be better off in the Wilkerson mansion than with me, I wouldn't stand in the way. But material possessions aren't of much value compared to personal love and caring...and eternal salvation."

"Oh, so we're back to that. Religion." Guy's snort was both frustrated and contemptuous. "It doesn't look to me as if your God is so loving and wonderful in the way he killed off Sylvia and Mark and left their baby an orphan."

In her first dark moments of despair, that thought had also occurred to Beth. Even now she sometimes wondered why the Lord had chosen this tangled, painful path for all of them. The tragic deaths, her job and financial problems, and now this new threat. Was it possible the Lord would allow the Wilkersons to snatch Joey from her?

"If I had any Christian faith," Guy added, "I think what happened to Sylvia and Mark would be enough to shatter it."

"It hasn't shattered mine," Beth said resolutely. "The way the Lord works may be difficult to understand, but I know that his vision sees far beyond mine and that I can entrust both my earthly and eternal future to him."

Guy absentmindedly fingered the bandage, her words of faith bouncing off him unheeded. "Bethany, my father can be a formidable adversary," he said slowly. "What Nat Wilkerson wants, Nat gets. And if money isn't enough, he's willing to use...other means."

Beth caught her breath at the softly spoken warning. There was none of the domineering tone she'd heard earlier; this was simply a statement of fact.

"By going to court, you mean? A lawsuit over custody?"

"Perhaps. But not necessarily."

The words hung there, like cocked pistols aimed at her heart. Her head whirled with ominous possibilities. Kidnapping? A not-so-accidental accident? She was all that stood between Nat Wilkerson and the grandson he desperately wanted.

She shook her head. "No. I can't believe he'd do anything illegal." In business, Nat Wilkerson might cut a few corners on ethics; Sylvia had believed that. But surely a man of his standing wouldn't resort to violence or lawbreaking! Reluctantly she added, "What happens when you go home and tell your father I've refused to give up his grandson?"

Guy laughed without humor. "First he'll call me some unsavory names and tell me what an incompetent idiot I am. Then, while he's trying to decide a next step, he'll probably get a judge to issue an order restraining you from taking the baby anywhere out of his reach."

"I'm not planning to go anywhere except to my new job in Oklahoma City."

"And if the case does come to a court battle, don't expect it to be conducted on some high and lofty level. You'll find your name and reputation dragged through the mud, because that's how he'll try to get to you, by showing you're an unfit mother."

"I'm not an unfit mother! Do *you* think I'm an unfit mother?"

"What I think doesn't matter. Bethany, if you've ever so much as kissed a man, the lawyers will make you look like a...back street tramp. If you've ever had a mild romance, it will show up as a steamy affair."

Bethany shook her head in dismay. "I can't believe that!"

"Believe it. It was the first thing Nat said I should investigate about you, if you resisted giving us custody."

Beth swallowed. She'd never had a steamy affair, but she had gone to movies over in Warden and an occasional dance with various local young men, although that was all before she had the full-time responsibility of Joey. Could an unethical lawyer build something out of those innocent occasions?

"But there's something else." Guy paused, his gaze absent-mindedly studying the row of empty buildings as if searching for a spy lurking behind a boarded-up window. "You're a person whom I'm sure would never resort to unethical or underhanded tactics. But don't let your own goodness make you misjudge someone else's capabilities. Even if my father is certain he can win a legal battle, if he suspects that it could drag on for months, he'll resort to other tactics. Nat Wilkerson didn't get where he is by always playing by the rules."

These words, too, hung in the silent air, more powerful as a quiet warning than a shouted threat.

"What, exactly, is *your* position in the family business?" Beth asked. The other brother, who, Beth recalled, was several years older than Sylvia and Guy, was some sort of money manager or accountant for the family's business holdings.

Guy shifted in the luxurious seat as if the question made him uncomfortable. "I handle various details of personal and company matters," he said finally. "General troubleshooter, I suppose you might call it."

"Do you still drive race cars?"

"Sylvia told you that, too?"

"She was very fond of you, more sorry about the break with you than with her father or other brother, I believe. Although she always prayed for all of you."

A muscle twitched in Guy's angular jaw, as if her words

about Sylvia's feelings and prayers had affected him, but after a moment's silence he dismissed them without comment and went back to her question. "No, I've given up race-car driving. I really haven't time for it, and it was never more than a reckless hobby anyway, not a lifetime ambition."

And what, Beth wondered curiously, were his lifetime ambitions? To become another Nat Wilkerson?

"Look, you think this over, and we'll talk about it again in the morning. I'm sure we can work out something agreeable. Perhaps I could even suggest to Nat that you be hired as Joseph's nanny."

"A Christian nanny?" It was a Christian governess, Beth knew, who had first led Sylvia…and Guy…to Christ.

Guy smiled wryly. "Nat does become a bit inflamed on the subject of religion. But we'll discuss this again tomorrow."

Beth didn't see how a new day would change anything, but there seemed no point in arguing further now. Guy also needed to get into a hotel room where he could lie down and rest. She opened the door so she could get out and collect Joey from the backseat, but Guy reached across her and pulled the door shut.

"You take the car. I'll walk over to your house in the morning."

He slid out the passenger's door and grabbed the suitcase from the backseat. Why, she wondered as she watched him stride across the street to the hotel, had he told her all that about his father? A warning, obviously, of the dangers of defying the Wilkersons' power and money, and yet she had the unexpected feeling that it was not so much a ploy to achieve his own ends as an actual concern for her welfare. And it had been considerate of him to let her keep the car and not have to walk home carrying Joey.

For a moment the angle of the streetlights gave Guy's turban-bandage an almost halo-like glow, an ethereal image quickly dispelled when he banged the bell on the counter in the lobby, apparently with sufficient arrogance to startle several elderly, dozing occupants. And whatever he said made the hotel clerk, Orville Thompkins, known more for his good nature than his speed, jump with unaccustomed alacrity to pick up Guy's suitcase.

No, a halo was not the appropriate headgear for Guy Wilkerson.

Three

Beth stopped at the post office before going home. A single letter angled a diagonal silhouette across her glass-windowed mailbox...but it was the one she had been waiting for!

She caught her breath. She read the typewritten words once, then read them again in shocked disbelief.

There was no job! Because of financial problems, the school had decided to distribute the students among other classrooms rather than hire a replacement teacher. They "regretted any inconvenience."

Beth slumped against the wall. *Inconvenience?* She'd counted on this job! She'd peeked through the door of opportunity and seen a steady paycheck, security for her and Joey, even the possibility of taking art classes at the nearby university. Now the door had slammed so hard she could almost feel the floor shudder beneath her feet.

This wasn't fair! A rare anger stormed through her. She crumpled the letter and slammed the crushed ball into a wastepaper basket.

A moment later, unfairness faded into irrelevance compared

with the larger significance of this rejection. From the door of the post office she peered apprehensively at the hotel down the street, where a single light shone from the third floor like a malevolent eye. If the Wilkersons found out about this, found there was no job and no prospect of one...

Back home, she automatically fed and bathed Joey, glad he could now drink plain milk rather than the canned-milk formula the doctor had prescribed when there was no mother's milk for him. She nuzzled his baby-sweet body and played with him before tucking him into the crib, the love she felt for him heightened by the threat hanging over them. She kissed his feet and watched him squirm and laugh in delight. Losing Joey would tear out half her heart!

Beth warmed a bowl of leftover stew for her own supper, restlessly pacing back and forth as she ate. She had long known Nat Wilkerson was a hard, godless man, but Guy's hint of dangers beyond a legal battle stunned her. Was he really implying kidnap or physical harm?

What was she going to do now? She turned to the refuge she always sought when faced with problems or uncertainties. She went to the Lord.

She settled into the rocking chair with her Bible, browsing the words of wisdom that were as meaningful and powerful today as when written so long ago. She would have liked to find instructions emblazoned in neon so she couldn't possibly miss them, but, as was so often the Lord's way, his messages were more subtle. Over and over she found words of reassurance. From Hebrews, "I will never leave thee, nor forsake thee." From Samuel, "He is my shield, and the horn of my salvation, my high tower, and my refuge."

Yet she also kept coming across stories of departure, of walking with the Lord into the unknown. Ruth, following her mother-in-law into a strange land. Moses, leading his people toward a land they had never seen. Even Paul, on that fateful road to Damascus, was going somewhere. What was this saying to her?

Go?

She couldn't simply *go*, she scoffed. Where would she go? The job in Oklahoma City had vanished. *Why* would she go? She was just as vulnerable to the Wilkersons' money and power elsewhere as here. Indeed, even if she ignored all that, *how* would she go? Run off in Guy's elegant Packard? A fine chance she'd have of keeping Joey if she was in jail for car theft!

Yet she wasn't totally without material resources.

Thoughtfully Beth went to the kitchen cupboard where, behind the flour canister, she kept the small wooden box decorated with a chipped painting of a girl in flower-brimmed hat. A faint fragrance of cedar drifted up when she lifted the lid. On top was a dark, old-fashioned brooch, and she held its cool stone to her cheek briefly, treasuring it not for any monetary value, because it had little, but because it had belonged to her beloved grandmother.

Underneath were the few photographs that linked her to the past: Mark and Sylvia on their wedding day, both radiant with love; Beth the day she graduated from her teacher's training at Normal School; Beth and Mark when they were children, Beth curled inside the old tire Grandpa had hung from a branch in the tiny backyard of the St. Louis house, Mark balancing on top of the tire with arms outstretched and a reckless grin on his face. In another photo, Beth was perched atop a pyramid of girlhood friends, her own grin reckless.

There was a photo of Grandpa and Grandma sitting together in the swing rocker on the front porch, hands affectionately clasped, looking smaller and more fragile than Beth remembered them. There was an even older formal photo of the mother who had died when Beth was four. Her memories of her mother were dim: a sweet laugh, a faint fragrance of rose-scented cologne, a tired embrace after a long day's work at some factory. There were neither photos nor memories of the father who had abandoned the family when Beth was only two.

But she'd never been deprived, she thought almost fiercely. Not in the way Sylvia had been deprived in the Wilkerson mansion, raised by a series of loveless nannies and governesses. Grandpa's injury at the mill had left him unable to do more than odd jobs, and her grandmother took in washing and sewing, but Beth and Mark's upbringing had been rich in love and laughter and strong Christian faith.

Beneath the photographs was Sylvia's letter. Beth would have eagerly assumed responsibility for Joey even if the letter had never been written, but she'd always appreciated Sylvia and Mark's confidence in her. At the very bottom of the box lay the leather pouch with drawstring top. She balanced it lightly on her palm, not needing to count the bills to know to the dollar how much the pouch contained.

Several times in the past two months it had seemed as if she surely must dip into this small inheritance from her grandfather, but each time a day or two of tutoring or a gift of food or supplies—once an unexpected commission to do a baby portrait—had managed to sustain her and Joey a little longer. Because the Lord was preserving the money for this particular time of need, she wondered?

To be used how? To battle the Wilkersons in court? It would, she thought grimly, run out before the Wilkersons used up their spare change. But, she mused, the money could be sufficient for something else entirely.

No! What good would leaving Ryman Springs do? Her

problems would simply go with her.

But what if the Wilkersons couldn't *find* her?

She would think about this later, she told herself firmly as she put everything back in the cedar box.

No. Go *now*. Now, before Nat Wilkerson got some judge to order her to turn Joey over to him. Before he took even more drastic and sinister steps to claim his grandson.

Slowly, reluctantly, she walked through the small house, studying her few possessions from a new and shivery perspective.

There were things she'd hate to leave behind. The pendulum clock that had belonged to her grandparents. The old cane-bottomed rocker in which she'd rocked Joey to sleep so many times. The crib Mark had lovingly built when his child was yet unborn. But what was really essential? Baby things for Joey. The contents of the cedar box. A few clothes and personal belongings for herself. Her Bible.

She glanced at the face of the pendulum clock hanging on the wall, its rhythmic tick-tock suddenly a giant gallop in the silence. In three hours the midnight train would chug into Ryman Springs. Could she simply *go* and trust the Lord to lead her to a haven safe from the Wilkersons? In spite of a lifetime of faith and trust, the thought tightened her throat with alarm.

The Wilkersons would find her. A woman and baby couldn't simply disappear. And the money wouldn't last long. How could she actually go through with this?

The powerful words from Psalms didn't come with a red blaze of neon, but they came, marching into her mind like sturdy soldiers. *Thou art my hiding place and my shield.*

Go.

She worked swiftly, intent on speed rather than cautious deliberation. Joey's things went in the scarred valise, her belongings in a battered suitcase. She spooned the pureed baby food she'd prepared earlier into jars and filled baby bottles with fresh milk, putting these items for immediate usage into a big cloth bag with a sturdy shoulder strap. Quickly, before fear of the unknown could stop her, she carried everything out to the Packard, dwelling only briefly on the irony of this Wilkerson aid in her escape.

As she put the seldom-used key on the table and studied the faded wallpaper, battered furniture, and leak-stained ceiling for one last time, raw panic clutched her. The tiny teacher's cottage wasn't much, but it had been home, safe and secure, and the school board had assured her she could live here as long as she wanted.

Maybe what she was doing wasn't of the Lord; maybe it was just a wild, hot-headed mistake....

Go.

Beth was relieved when she found the railroad station empty except for the stationmaster, old LaMar Miner. She felt bad about leaving without telling anyone goodbye, but the fewer witnesses and explanations the better. She settled Joey on a wooden bench and tucked the suitcase and valise around him to keep him from rolling off. She approached the iron-barred window slowly. Where was she going on this wild midnight escape?

Yet tonight's destination didn't really matter, she realized. Because it was only the first leg of some longer journey.

"Oklahoma City, please," she finally said to LaMar.

She'd already told Guy she had a job in Oklahoma City—he might waste time searching for her there, time that *she* could use to put more miles between them. LaMar licked a finger and reached into a cubbyhole beside the window, as usual, not in any great hurry.

"How's Emmaline doing?" Beth inquired.

LaMar's granddaughter had come down with a paralysis two summers ago, and Beth had for weeks given her special at-home lessons until the family moved to Texas.

"Oh, middlin'," LaMar said. "But we just praise the Lord she's still with us. And for all the help you gave her." He laboriously started making out the ticket. "Going on a visit, Miss Beth?"

"No, unfortunately I'm...moving away."

"We heard you might be leavin' us." LaMar glanced up from the ticket. "We're right sorry to see you go."

"I'm sorry to leave," she said, which was true. Even though she had never been able to love the stark plains wholeheartedly, she had loved the good people here. She half-expected LaMar to comment on her out-of-town visitor, but that bit of gossip apparently hadn't made the rounds yet. "I brought my luggage in a borrowed car. Could I prevail on you to watch Joey while I return it? I doubt he'll even wake up."

She'd thought about simply leaving the Packard at the station. Guy would figure out sooner or later that the train was the only way she could have slipped out of town. But without the clue of the car, that realization might come later rather than sooner, giving her extra minutes or hours of escape time.

"Sure thing, Miss Beth." LaMar beamed as if she'd awarded him some special honor.

With last-minute inspiration Beth added, "I had an out-of-town visitor today, and I'd prefer he not know where I've gone. Or, for that matter, that I've gone anywhere." She knew LaMar must be curious about details of this request, but he was too gentlemanly to ask. "He's simply someone I'd prefer never to see again," she added, which, if not particularly enlightening for LaMar, was certainly true.

"He won't hear nothin' from me." LaMar solemnly pretended to button his lips. "He won't hear from me if they was even a train come through here tonight."

Beth smiled and thanked him. She drove to the cottage, left the keys to the car on the front seat, and conscientiously made certain the doors and windows were tightly shut so snow couldn't blow in. There was no moon, but between snowy ground and pale clouds the night seemed to have an uneasy light of its own. By the time she hurried back to the station on foot, every moment breathless with a sudden fear that Guy would rush out of the hotel and stop her, the train whistle wailed at the first road crossing just outside of town.

She'd always liked hearing that midnight whistle from the snug security of her bed. It gave her dreamy thoughts of faraway city lights—Los Angeles and New York, New Orleans and Chicago. But tonight the sound filled her with a nervous blend of apprehension and anticipation. Because now she wasn't just dreaming of faraway places; she was actually leaving Ryman Springs.

She reached the station just as the train pulled in, and for a few moments, as the wooden platform rumbled beneath her feet, she fought an irrational, childish fear of this great snorting iron monster charging out of the night, all lights and noise and belching smoke, great churning wheels and clanking bell, hissing steam and screeching brakes. There was a certain unreality to it, as if some mechanical dragon had come to fire-breathing life.

And then she was too busy giving the conductor her ticket and getting her awkward collection of luggage and baby on board to give any thought to frivolous fears.

No one else got on or off, and the engineer didn't dawdle in this windswept corner of nowhere. Beth barely had her baggage stowed before they were moving. The coach swayed gently as the engine picked up speed, and the whistle blew again at the second road crossing.

Her last view of Ryman Springs, when she pressed her nose against the window in order to see through her own reflection in the glass, was the dark hulk of the hotel. Had she left any clues that would reveal her final destination to Guy Wilkerson?

No, no clues.

Because *she* didn't know where she was going.

The slow-moving hotel clerk set Guy's suitcase on a carpet that looked like a tired twin to the one in Bethany Curtis's little house. The room held one bed with a faded rose spread, one bureau with a cracked mirror, one chair, one nightstand, and one wastebasket.

However, after the last three months spent living in a dirt-floored tent on a Texas oilfield, it wasn't all that bad, Guy thought philosophically.

"Bathroom's two doors down the hall."

"Hot water?"

"Well, uh, sometimes."

Without bothering to undress, Guy stretched out on the lumpy bed, gingerly resting his bandaged head on the yellowed pillowcase. The throbbing pain had subsided to a dull ache, but he felt incredibly weary. He had, he thought wryly, put in fourteen-hour days at rough labor on an oil-drilling rig that were less debilitating than one afternoon in combat with Bethany Curtis.

And he'd thought all he had to do was wave a few bucks at her, add a mild threat or two, and she'd rip that custody paper out of his hand in eagerness to sign it! Instead, here he was, stuck in a fleabag of a hotel in Oklahoma, with a head that felt as if it had been attacked by a runaway sewing machine, a cashmere coat ruined by bloodstains, and nothing settled.

Reluctantly, Guy conceded a certain admiration for Bethany Curtis. She was not what he had expected, neither in terms of her stubborn determination to keep baby Joseph nor in her defiance of Wilkerson money and power. And she definitely was not what he'd expected in appearance.

Knowing Bethany Curtis was both a schoolteacher and a minister's sister, he'd expected a meek, plain, shapeless little church mouse. Her clothing indeed matched his expectations; he'd never seen such awful stockings! But when she'd stood with the wind from the open door molding her skirt and sweater against her slim body, her chin lifted defiantly, she was definitely not shapeless. And that spectacular cascade of auburn hair! Plus blazing blue eyes, a surprising physical strength when she helped him to his feet, and a sweet dusting of twelve faint, rosy-tan freckles across her cheeks and nose.

How did he know how many freckles? Because he'd counted them! He couldn't recall ever before counting any woman's freckles. Although that could be, he thought, because most women he knew wouldn't dream of letting a freckle escape a concealing layer of paint and powder. Or was it because Bethany Curtis intrigued him in a way no other woman ever had?

He hadn't been eager to make this trip to Oklahoma to claim his father's only grandchild. Now that he'd met Bethany, he had even greater doubts about taking Joseph away from her. It was true that the Wilkersons could provide material benefits far beyond anything Bethany could offer. He didn't doubt her claim of Sylvia's letter entrusting the baby to her, and he wasn't convinced Joseph would be better off in the St. Louis mansion. He'd told Bethany that his brother's wife would take a motherly interest in the baby, but somehow he couldn't see social-climbing Carolyn giving up any of her shopping, bridge games, or fancy dinners to devote time and attention to Joseph. And Guy well remembered his own childhood that had known none of the warmth and affection Bethany showered on her little nephew.

His younger sister Sylvia was all that had kept that childhood from desperate loneliness. Their older brother Warren was almost as distant a figure as their father, but Guy and Sylvia were just a year apart in age. No matter how remote their father and brother were, how often the governesses changed, or how cold and authoritarian they were, he and Sylvia always had each other with whom to laugh and play and get into mischief. Two little rich kids against the world, he thought now with a certain wry sadness. Then Mrs. Sommersby had come, the most wonderful governess they'd ever had, bringing a surprising combination of fun and love and Jesus. But Nat, infuriated when Sylvia tried to share their newfound faith with him, had fired Mrs. Sommersby and shipped Sylvia and Guy off to separate boarding schools.

For a moment an old anger at that injustice flared inside Guy. An anger intensified when he recalled how Nat hadn't even notified him when Sylvia died. He'd been at the resort hotel down in Florida, straightening out some management problems, and the funeral was long over by the time he returned to St. Louis. He'd have defied his father and gone if he'd known, which was why Nat hadn't told him, of course. Death did not soften Nat Wilkerson's harsh views. Sylvia had rebelled in life, and he would not forgive her in death.

Sometimes Guy was half inclined to tell Nat he was dropping out of the family business empire and heading out on his own. To Bethany he'd called himself a "general troubleshooter," and that was true, but his basic job was doing his father's dirty work, *making* trouble, firing or threatening or investigating. That was why he'd spent three months incognito on the oil field, finding out what was happening to several thousand barrels of Wilkerson oil that were disappearing every month. And nailing the culprit with his hands practically black with oil.

But this was never supposed to have been his full-time career. Back at boarding school he'd worked on the school newspaper and loved it, and he had looked forward to going into journalism. Nat, however, had wanted him to get a prestigious Harvard education that he felt would be of greater value to the family financial empire, asserting that later he'd buy a newspaper and Guy could run it.

Well, here he was, seven years out of college, and the only time he'd gotten near a newspaper was when Nat had sent him to threaten a local publisher with financial disaster if some ugly details about a certain real estate deal appeared in print.

Restlessly, but cautiously, Guy changed position on the bed, grimacing as the stitches pulled like small claws at the back of his scalp. All this ruminating about the past was getting him nowhere. He had a problem to solve.

Not really such a complicated problem after all, he decided. The solution was simply for Bethany to come to St. Louis as Joseph's nanny. Joseph would then have both the benefits of the Wilkerson wealth and Bethany's loving care. She'd instantly targeted the big barrier to that idea: Nat's raw hostility toward Christian beliefs. But Bethany would need to keep her religious views to herself, and he would need to convince Nat that she'd never shared her minister brother's beliefs.

From Guy's personal point of view, the prospect of having Bethany in the St. Louis mansion held an intriguing appeal as well.

Guy slept then, intending only to take a brief nap before

going out to eat, but he didn't waken until the middle of the night when a train whistle rattled him awake. His head throbbed again, and he staggered down the hall for a glass of water with which to take two more pills. They churned uncomfortably in his empty stomach, and he sat on the edge of the bed for several minutes, keeping them down with pure will power. He was just drifting back to sleep when a second wail of the train whistle roused him again.

He raised up on one elbow with a brief, inexplicable ripple of uneasiness, as if the whistle were telling him something important. But that was ridiculous, of course. It was just a midnight train, here in the middle of nowhere. He went back to sleep.

In the morning, despite empty stomach, tender head, and a lukewarm bath and shave, he felt reasonably chipper. He discarded the bloodied white shirt and cashmere coat and dressed in dark slacks and a knit sweater he'd picked up in Italy a few years ago. He lingered over an excellent ham and eggs breakfast at the Ryman Springs Café, giving Bethany plenty of time to contemplate what he'd said yesterday before offering her his plan for compromise.

He strolled to her house at about ten o'clock. It was a fine morning, icy but blue-skied and sunny. He knocked, then knocked again when there was no response.

He stepped back and looked at the window in which he'd first seen her yesterday. The blue rag she'd been stuffing in a drafty crack still dangled there, framed by ruffled yellow curtains she'd undoubtedly made herself in an attempt to brighten her surroundings.

The words and even a bit of tune from some old song Mrs. Sommersby had taught them unexpectedly came back to him: *Brighten the corner where you are...* Odd that he'd remember it, after all these years.

What had happened to those beliefs about Jesus and salvation he'd shared with Sylvia and Mrs. Sommersby? He'd never experienced any dramatic shattering of faith, but somehow, at boarding school, and later, in the sophisticated milieu of college, it had all simply drifted into irrelevance.

Sylvia had tried to talk to him when they were home together for holidays, but he'd just ruffled her hair affectionately and told her he'd outgrown all that. He'd been a lonely, naïve kid when he'd...what was the phrase? "Accepted Christ." A boy with a boy's fears and inexperience and weakness. Now he was a man, capable and self-sufficient. Religion was a myth invented to fortify the weak, he'd proclaimed to Sylvia with superior worldliness, echoing a cynical professor he'd heard at college.

Guy walked out to the car, saw the keys on the seat, and decided to drive down to the store; if Bethany was on an errand, carrying the baby, she'd appreciate a lift home.

Bethany was not at the store; the clerk said he hadn't seen her that morning. Neither had the postmaster. Perhaps she'd gone to visit someone, he decided. She was undoubtedly the kind of woman who took chicken soup to ill neighbors and visited housebound old ladies. He drove back to the small house and settled back to wait.

He'd drifted off to sleep, he realized, when he jerked awake and found to his surprise that it was almost one o'clock. Clouds blotted the sun now. Still no answer when he knocked on the door. On impulse, he pushed it open, in the silence hearing a squeak he hadn't noticed before. "Bethany?"

No answer. He turned and looked back toward the car. For the first time, he noticed the absence of any fresh footprints but his own in the windblown snow. A faint alarm stirred inside him.

He stepped inside. The house was cold. Frigid. He touched

the metal stove. There had been no fire in it for hours.

The alarm expanded. The bedroom door was open. He hesitated briefly, feeling like an unwelcome intruder. He strode to the door anyway.

The bed had not been slept in. The crib was empty, stripped to bare mattress. The few well-worn items in the closet had a forlorn, abandoned look. He returned to the living room, now aware of something other than physical coldness in the air—an indefinable emptiness, as if some essence of warmth and life were missing.

Bethany's warmth, Bethany's life....

The alarm ballooned in a different direction, to a startling new possibility. He instantly scoffed at the idea. Impossible. She couldn't simply pick up and disappear overnight. She was encumbered with a baby. She had no financial resources, no car.

Then he saw the key on the oak table, and the alarm exploded into incredulous fury.

She *was* gone! Sneaked out. Vanished. And she'd taken baby Joseph with her! He knew it as surely as if she'd left a taunting goodbye note. But where would she go? *How* would she go?

A midnight memory floated back to him, a lonesome whistle. The train.

Four

The train stopped at what seemed to Beth must surely be every chicken coop, water tower, and one-horse town in the state. They were shuffled off to a siding for an interminable wait. She mentally groaned with each delay.

By the time the train reached Oklahoma City, an icy morning sun greeted her as a porter carried her luggage into the station. She glanced around cautiously, reasonably certain Guy couldn't be here waiting to pounce on her, but jumpy anyway. Now what?

Hide here? No. Better to put more miles between herself and Guy Wilkerson as quickly as possible. She studied the confusing list of names and times on the chalk-printed board. In spite of ragged nerves and lack of sleep, Beth felt an unexpected exhilaration as possible destinations beckoned like flirtatious suitors.

New Orleans…southern mansions, gulf breezes, magnolias. Very appealing! Memphis…paddle steamers on the Mississippi, lush green fields, ladies in gaily flowered hats. Tempting!

But the high-spirited moment vanished as the name of St.

Louis caught her eye. St. Louis, the lair of the Wilkersons, whose web of money and power could stop her in her tracks if she were not shrewd and wily enough to elude them.

She abandoned her dreamy contemplation of appealing destinations and studied departure times only: 3:20 P.M.; 4:15 P.M.; 11:45 A.M. No, no, no. She couldn't risk sitting here all that time. But there...8:12 A.M.! She couldn't think of any recommendation for Ft. Worth, Texas, but at the moment the immediate departure time was sufficient.

Within minutes, Oklahoma City was receding behind them. Beth felt more free with each passing mile on the swaying train. With the clue of her "job" to guide him, Guy would mire down in a fruitless search for her in Oklahoma City, and she and Joey would be miles away!

Her arrival in Ft. Worth went smoothly. With the aid of a taxi driver, she soon had a room at a boarding house, plus arrangements for the landlady to care for Joey while she looked for a job.

She spent the next day putting in applications for various teaching positions. The following day she answered newspaper advertisements and canvassed shops and offices. She had just left a downtown lawyer's office, buoyed by a tiny bit of encouragement, when an elegant, all-too-familiar-looking automobile braked at a stoplight not a dozen feet from her. She stopped short, fighting instant panic and a thunder of heartbeat in her ears, then shakily reassuring herself that she was wildly overreacting; there were undoubtedly *hundreds* of sleek silver Packards in existence.

But surely not more than one driven by a rugged-shouldered man with a turban-bandage wrapped around a rough fringe of gold-bronze hair!

Beth frantically darted back through the revolving door of

the building. She waited a solid ten minutes before daring to venture out and then, rather than risk the exposure of walking back to the boarding house, hailed a cab.

Back in the haven of her room, she felt as if she had barely escaped the snap of a bear trap. This changed everything. How had it happened? No one but the ticket-seller and perhaps a porter knew she had come to Ft. Worth. But they had no reason to remember her.

She glanced up as she paced nervously between bed and bureau. She stopped short at the sight of her own disheveled reflection in the mirror.

Beth had never thought of herself as some traffic-stopping beauty; she didn't now. Yet as she stared at her reflection in the mirror she had to admit that she and Joey together were a bit out of the ordinary. She could almost hear Guy saying, with a finger poised over his wallet promising a reward for helpful information, "I'm trying to locate a young woman traveling with a seven-month-old baby. She has long, rather noticeable auburn hair. Have you seen her?"

She must be much more clever and devious than she had been so far. And get a lot farther away than she was now.

A disguise? Age herself with matronly clothes, glasses, hair stuffed under a prim hat? From which it would no doubt come tumbling down at some awkward and incriminating moment.

With one hand Beth slowly gathered and lifted the rich cascade of red-brown hair shimmering with fiery highlights. She stretched it out to full length and slowly let it drop. She shook her head in silent protest. Not her hair! She hadn't cut it since she was thirteen years old. She remembered the coziness of her grandmother brushing it every night, and how a sweet-talking beau had once called it "sunset silk."

She swallowed harshly and turned away from the mirror.

The hair was a dead giveaway, and she must not let foolish vanity jeopardize their escape from the Wilkersons.

At the boarding house dining table, she carefully planted the misinformation that she had decided to go north to Chicago to look for work. After dinner, door locked, she extracted a pair of tiny scissors from a manicure set Sylvia had given her and started cutting. She didn't watch her reflection in the mirror, simply gnawed away until a puddle of shimmering auburn surrounded her on the floor and her head felt weightless and naked.

When she finally looked, she was torn between tears and laughter. Her hair was no "crowning glory" now. No, it was a strange stubble of mismatched lengths, with odd little tufts and stubs sticking up here and there, and her exposed ears looked large and ungainly. Quickly, before tears could sink the laughter, she gathered the loose hair into a page of newspaper and stuffed it in her suitcase. She mustn't leave that giveaway clue behind to arouse someone's curiosity!

Next morning, with a scarf hiding her shorn head, she walked the dozen blocks to a secondhand store. There, gaily chattering about a brother needing clothes for a family gathering, she made her purchases.

Back in her room, the boy's clothing turned out to be too large, and definitely an awkward fit on her feminine figure, but she shortened the pant legs and jacket sleeves and filled the toes of the shoes with leftover scraps of fabric. Then she stuck the tweed cap on her head, added the glasses, and cautiously eyed herself in the mirror.

She blinked and peered again, because what looked for all the world like a studious adolescent boy was staring back at her. An adolescent boy in an ill-fitting suit, with a haircut that looked as if it had been done with a butcher knife on a dark night, but an adolescent boy nevertheless!

Next morning, dressed in a dark skirt and blouse, with her lack of hair again concealed by an artfully arranged scarf, Beth carefully confided to the landlady that the ex-husband who had beaten her might come looking for her, and if he did she fervently hoped the landlady wouldn't give him any helpful information. She shivered under the weight of all these wild fabrications, so far removed from her honest Christian nature, but she saw no other way.

The landlady then gave a bit of unexpected assistance, offering the services of a nephew to drive Beth to the bus station, from which, in a further effort to muddy her trail, she had said she was departing. There, in the ladies' lavatory, she changed to her boy's outfit, an awkward maneuver made doubly difficult while juggling baby Joey in the cramped stall. Feeling uncomfortable and none too convincing in her disguise, she then took a taxi to the train station.

There, tweed cap pulled low on her head, she sidled up to the ticket window. "Los Angeles, please," she muttered to the wavy face of the ticket-seller. The glasses were far more distorting than she had first realized, and the undulating images made her feel almost seasick.

"That's a long way for two young fellers to be going alone, sonny." The ticket-seller eyed Beth and Joey with disapproving suspicion.

Beth wavered between exhilaration that the disguise was working—he'd called her "sonny"!—and panic that the man apparently suspected her of being anything from a runaway to a kidnapper.

"My big sister Ellen already got her ticket. See? That's her sittin' over there. Me 'n' her 'n' my little brother here are gonna go live with our gramma." Beth waved toward a row of people sitting on a nearby bench, hoping one of them looked like a sister

Ellen. "All she can think about is *boys*," Beth added irrelevantly, feigning a disgust that apparently convinced the man of the authenticity of this arrangement because he laughed and started making out the ticket.

Then, that precious passport to escape safely in hand, Beth picked an inconspicuous corner bench and settled down to wait. All she had to do now was make herself and Joey invisible for the next two hours, until the train pulled out of the station.

And hope she never saw Guy Wilkerson again.

Guy bypassed his own office and headed upstairs to his father's top-floor suite. He may as well get this over with immediately.

"Nat in?" he inquired of his father's stout, long-time secretary.

"I'll let him know you're here," Mrs. Exeter said. No one, not even his sons, simply barged into Nat Wilkerson's office.

Guy rotated his stiff shoulders and crossed to the window rather than sit on the leather sofa. He'd had more than enough sitting on the long drive up from Ft. Worth. He'd come by St. Louis's "Hooverville," the name given to the rough settlements of homeless people springing up around big cities everywhere these days, and the scene had left him troubled. He was tired, frustrated with his futile search for Bethany Curtis, and angry that she had deceived and outwitted him. Yet at the same time he felt a grudging admiration and respect for her courage and determination and cleverness.

"Mr. Wilkerson will see you now," the secretary announced with her customary formality.

Nat, white shirt-sleeves rolled up and muscular forearms spread on a cluttered desk, looked up when Guy entered. His father's hair was more gray than gold-bronze now, and he had gained some beefy weight over the years, but there was nothing soft, flabby, or age-weakened about him. His gray eyes still glinted with cold steel. Irrelevantly, Guy wondered if his own eyes had looked like that to Bethany.

Nat glanced at the grimy bandage on Guy's head. "What happened to you?"

"A minor accident. A few stitches."

Nat didn't waste time with sympathy or concern. "You have the signed custody papers?"

"She refused to sign."

"I didn't send you down there on a joyride!" Papers flew as Nat's fist slammed against the desk. "I sent you there for *results.*"

Guy suppressed a quick spike of his own anger at his father's instant, arrogant anger. "She refuses even to consider releasing the child to us. I put considerable pressure on her—"

"Apparently not enough." Nat, ever a man of quick action, or intolerance for failure, reached for the black candlestick telephone on his desk.

Guy put a restraining hand on the instrument. "Wait. Before you call the lawyer…" He hesitated, not certain it wasn't someone even more disreputable than that legal shark Boydston whom his father intended to call. Then, knowing the glacial reception his next words would probably receive, he barged on.

"Miss Curtis is an extremely responsible and caring young woman, very capable and obviously devoted to the baby." This was something he'd thought about all the way home, a silent argument he'd resolutely separated from his feelings of frustration and anger at being outmaneuvered and outwitted. With Bethany he'd parroted the family line of marvelous advantages for Joseph in the Wilkersons' custody, but after an honest weighing of what was truly best for Joseph, he now found himself repeating Bethany's own words. "The baby is healthy, happy, and in good hands with her. I think we should simply let him remain there."

The idea brought no more than a blink of hostile surprise from Nat. He dismissed it with the same arrogance he treated any opinion conflicting with his own. "I want my grandson."

"Miss Curtis has a letter from Sylvia authorizing her to raise the baby. And specifically stating that we are *not* to have him."

If his daughter's rejection of him as a caretaker for his grandson had any effect on Nat, his granite expression did not reveal it. "I'm going to get him."

"There's a...complication."

"She's a backwoods schoolteacher," Nat snorted contemptuously. "She hasn't a snowball's chance in a blast furnace against us."

"She's disappeared."

That statement, unlike the information about his daughter's rejection, apparently jolted Nat. He half rose from his chair, arms ramrod straight above hands planted stiffly against the desk. "What do you mean, disappeared?"

"I mean, she's disappeared. Vanished. She simply picked up, bag, baggage and baby, and sneaked out of town in the middle of the night."

Briefly Guy explained how he had immediately driven to Oklahoma City after concluding Bethany had fled Ryman Springs on the midnight train, a conclusion reached without any assistance from that tight-lipped stationmaster. A glimpse of a fifty-dollar bill had widened the stubborn old codger's eyes but done nothing to loosen his tongue.

"Once there, I discovered she'd immediately gone on to Ft. Worth." That had been easy. He'd simply inquired of the ticket-sellers if anyone had seen a beautiful young woman traveling with a baby, a woman with flaming auburn hair cascading to her waist, and he'd learned quickly enough that she'd bought a ticket to Ft. Worth.

"And then?"

"After three days chasing around Ft. Worth interrogating taxi drivers—" A bit of dogged detective work of which he was rather proud. "—I finally found one who had taken her to a boarding house."

With the foreknowledge of unsigned custody papers, Nat was not impressed. "And then?"

"And then she vanished. The landlady at the boarding house wouldn't admit Miss Curtis had even been there, although I'm sure she did stay there a night or two." The landlady had also looked at *him* as if she were considering doing even more lethal damage to his bandaged head. "After that, I couldn't find anyone who remembered seeing her."

Nat steepled his fingers, an ominous gesture. "You're telling me you carelessly let this woman *and* my grandson slip through your fingers and now you have absolutely no idea where they are."

"I wouldn't call it careless," Guy protested uncomfortably.

With his usual short-fused lack of interest in excuses, Nat cut Guy off with a growled command. "Get a detective on it. I don't want my grandson trapped in the hands of some wild-eyed, Bible-spouting religious fanatic. And I don't want any more clumsy, incompetent delays."

Guy slowly straightened in the chair. The "incompetent" and "clumsy" were aimed at him, but he'd been called worse. It was the scornful attack on Bethany that rattled the already taut cage of his nerves. She'd expressed a strong faith, true, but he'd seen nothing "fanatic" about her. Stiffly he said, "Miss Curtis is no wild-eyed fanatic."

"She's the sister of that ranting, raving, conniving preacher Sylvia married, isn't she?"

Guy doubted that was an accurate description of Mark Curtis, but it was irrelevant and he didn't argue the point. "Whatever her beliefs, I strongly suspect that Joseph is better off with Miss Curtis than he'd ever be with us. She wants to raise him because she loves him, not to fulfill some egotistical ambition for a family dynasty."

The steel of Nat's eyes glittered as if freshly sharpened, but he gave no other indication that he'd even heard Guy's harsh attack on both his motives and ego. "Call Blacketer. He's good. He got the evidence for us on that river property situation."

"Half that evidence was manufactured!"

"Tell him I don't care what it costs, I just want her found. As soon as he locates her, have him notify us and I'll decide how we'll go about rescuing the child."

"Rescuing? *Rescuing?* Is that how you plan to justify taking the baby?" The idea of "rescuing" Joseph from Bethany was so unfair, so ludicrous, that Guy jumped to his feet, frustrated and angry with his father's arrogant refusal even to consider any opposing point of view. "He doesn't need rescuing! He needs *us* to leave both him and Bethany alone, not hound them like a pack of wolves after a pair of lambs!"

"You're giving the orders around here now?" Nat inquired with dangerous delicacy.

Guy's jaw clenched. No, he wasn't giving the orders. Nat delegated duties, but he never let the *power* out of his hands. But neither, Guy vowed resolutely as his eyes locked with his father's, was he taking this particular order; no way was he going to sic some vulture of a detective on Bethany and baby Joseph.

Nat's steel-silver gaze didn't falter as his eyes clashed with Guy's, but unexpectedly he relaxed and laughed. "Bethany," he repeated, shrewdly catching the switch from the impersonal

Miss Curtis. "I'll bet she's a looker, right? And she wound you right around her little finger."

Guy hesitated, momentarily feeling foolish. Yes, Bethany was a "looker." Had he let himself be influenced by that? After all, Joseph *would* have many advantages in the Wilkerson mansion that he'd never have with Bethany.

Then he remembered the feel of the squirmy, inquisitive baby in his arms, so innocent and trusting, and Bethany hovering nearby, love and concern written all over her face, that beautiful face with its twelve freckles.

No. He wasn't backing down on this.

Nat shrugged. "Okay. Skip it." Briskly he added, "I want you to get out to the meat-packing plant immediately and see what's going on. I'm hearing rumors about union agitators making trouble there."

Guy started to protest. It was a three-hundred mile drive to the packing plant in Iowa. He needed to see a doctor about his head wound and a barber about his chopped-off hair. He needed a steaming-hot bath, a good meal, and a new overcoat.

But he *had* won the point about Bethany and the detective.

He glanced at his watch. "I suppose I can leave in a couple of hours." He stood up and started for the office door.

"Good. And as I said—"

Guy paused, suddenly wary at a certain smoothness in his father's voice. He turned and looked back. Nat was smiling complacently.

"As I said, don't bother about Blacketer. I'll contact him myself."

Nat Wilkerson might change techniques or tactics, Guy thought grimly as he turned on his heel and stalked to the door. He knew when to flaunt his power and when to alter his technique. But one way or another, what Nat wanted, Nat got.

J oey whimpered lightly. Beth gave him a quick kiss. Poor baby. Eating different food at odd hours and sleeping crowded together in an upper berth on the swaying train were a rough contrast to the comfortable routine and familiar crib he'd always known.

They both needed a bath, and Beth was thoroughly tired of the scratchy boy's suit and the strain of pretending she was Joey's big brother. But bath and abandonment of disguise would have to wait the several hundred miles yet to travel before they reached Los Angeles.

Minus the distorting spectacles, which she'd given up trying to include in her disguise, Beth stared restlessly at the seemingly endless, alien landscape of the southern Arizona desert. Huge cactuses spread thick arms as if in mysterious semaphoric signal. Other cactuses glowed with a halo of golden fuzz, while still others looked like long, thorny whips...or some land-locked octopi with heads buried in the sand! The parched ground stretched dry as old bones, and yet floodwaters had at some time left behind savage scars, bits of debris still clinging high in tree branches. It wasn't like the lush green farmland that she had always thought of as beautiful, and yet it had a harsh, alien beauty of its own, as if the Lord had experimented here with some different dimension of beauty.

The conductor interrupted Beth's thoughts as he strode through the cars announcing that the train would be arriving in Phoenix shortly. Beth was surprised as they approached the city to see the desert give way to irrigated green fields and canals sparkling with water. At the station, with Joey napping soundly, Beth stepped out to stretch her legs. She breathed deeply as she strolled the length of the train station, her nose catching an unlikely mixture of desert dryness and lush irrigated fields. Perhaps she should have chosen Phoenix as her destination, she thought as she closed her eyes and lifted her face to the unfamiliar warmth of January sunshine.

Her eyes flew open. Why not?

There was no reason she must continue on. In fact, there was an excellent reason *not* to go farther! If Guy managed to learn she'd bought a ticket for Los Angeles, that was where he'd look for her. He might even dash cross-country in his Packard and get there ahead of her. She could be rushing headlong into his snare!

With an impulsive recklessness of her own, Beth hurried back onto the train and wrestled her luggage from the rack. She lugged the heavy suitcase to the loading dock, made a second trip for the valise of Joey's things, and on the third brought Joey himself.

She plopped on the upright suitcase, breathless as much from the rash decision as the physical exertion. But unexpectedly that elated rush of glorious freedom surged through her again. She'd escaped, a prisoner no more! Guy would have no idea where she'd left the train. Now all she need do was find a place to live, get a job—not as a schoolteacher, of course, because Guy might try to trace her through work. And she couldn't go by her real name.

The exhilaration shriveled a bit as her list of problems expanded, and she felt a moment of pure panic when the windows of the train slid past with gathering speed, leaving her behind. She and Joey were alone here, alone in a strange desert city.

No, not alone, she corrected with a deep breath and calming flood of faith. Never alone. *I will never leave thee, nor forsake thee.* The Lord was here, just as he was in every corner of his creation. He'd brought her this far, and he wouldn't desert her now.

What she must do, she decided briskly, was simply tackle her problems in logical order. The first item was to transform herself from adolescent boy back to proper young lady. She was afraid this could be a complicated problem, but she caught the ladies' lavatory unoccupied during a lull between trains and made the switch. She emerged a bit rumpled, skirt and blouse wrinkled from their hiding place in the bottom of Joey's baby bag, but she was eminently female again. She was also, she thought ruefully as she glimpsed herself in the lavatory mirror, possessor of the world's most dreadful haircut. But hair would grow, she assured herself.

As if the Lord were clearing a pathway for her, everything fell neatly into place. Through a newspaper advertisement she found a clean and comfortable boarding house, the proprietor a good Christian woman whose warm heart belied her raw-boned figure and stern, ruddy face. She immediately took Beth and Joey under her wing as if they were motherless chicks and she a chick-less mother.

"Well, praise the Lord," Mrs. Welsch beamed as she accepted Beth's payment for a week's rent. "There hasn't been a baby under this roof in years."

"You don't have grandchildren?"

"No. Like you, I was widowed young. But you—! Losing your husband before this sweet baby was even born."

Beth squirmed guiltily at this unwarranted sympathy. She also felt a powerful stab of warning. It wasn't until Mrs. Welsch just now pointed out that the "husband" had died before Joey was born that Beth realized she'd carelessly come dangerously close to picking dates that wouldn't add up.

Her story was that she was Annie Thompson, Annie chosen from the last half of her own real name, Thompson from her grandparents. It was a name she thought her brain would not misplace at some incriminating moment. She was a widow from Seattle. Her schoolteacher husband, she claimed, had died a year ago from tuberculosis, and she had come to Phoenix because the doctor recommended the desert air for her own health. She'd intended to change Joey's name, but she'd already called him Joey to Mrs. Welsch, so it was too late for that. She nervously hoped no one would ask for too many details. Deception was not an area of expertise with her.

Beth received no encouragement from the various offices and businesses she contacted looking for work those first few days, Mrs. Welsch generously looking after Joey. But on Sunday, on the way home from church, Mrs. Welsch herself unexpectedly provided a job tip.

A friend had mentioned that her cousin Millie said she was going to quit her cooking and housekeeping job if she didn't get additional help with her employer's children. Millie's employer was a widower whose daughter and her two children had moved in with him after a divorce back East. The daughter was more interested in writing society news for her father's newspaper—along with chasing around looking for a new husband, Cousin Millie had complained—than she was in taking care of her children.

It seemed a tenuous job possibility, perhaps more gossip than fact, but Beth didn't intend to let even a flimsy possibility escape her. Mrs. Welsch obtained the name and address, and the following evening Beth walked to the much more prosperous area of town in which the Gardiner house was located.

Here the houses were large and the yards green with lawns and shrubs, as if the occupants were determined to keep the desert far at bay. The Gardiner house had an elegant peaked tower on one corner, gracefully arched windows, and a profusion of porches and balconies with wrought-iron railings.

The front door flew open just as Beth arrived. A sleek, dark-haired woman a few years older than Beth stepped out. She was wearing a narrow skirt and a fashionable, short fur jacket known as a "chubbie." She laughed vivaciously, head tilted provocatively toward the man following her. Before the door closed, Beth heard childish shrieks and an ominous-sounding thud. The woman didn't look back.

Beth's knock on a screen door at the rear of the house was eventually answered by a plump, aproned woman with limp wisps of gray hair and a harried expression. Two angelic-faced children about five years old peeked around her.

"Millie?" Beth inquired. The children, a girl in ruffled pink nightgown and a sturdy boy in blue pajamas, were so matching in size and looks that she knew they must be twins. "I understand there may be a job opening for a nanny or governess here."

The woman looked even more flustered, as if she hadn't anticipated that her grumbling would bring this response. "No, I don't think so."

"I found a scorpion today," the boy announced cheerfully to Beth.

"We put it in the stew," the little girl added helpfully.

Millie's eyes rounded with appalled horror. "You didn't!"

The two looked at each other and giggled, and Beth suspected they were making up this wild story simply to harass the housekeeper. However, as she watched the girl slyly maneuver to untie Millie's shoestrings with her bare toes, Beth reconsidered; perhaps these two really had seasoned the stew with a scorpion. And created that uproar.

Millie muttered, "Wait here," to Beth, grabbed each child by an arm and marched them into the house. A few minutes later she returned, still clutching the children like a policeman with a pair of runaways. Both her shoelaces were now untied. She jerked her head toward the interior of the house. "You can see Mr. Gardiner now."

Mr. Gardiner stood when Beth entered the book-lined den. He was short and wiry, with thinning gray hair and an expression only slightly less harried than the housekeeper's.

"I understand you may be in need of someone to help care for the children?" Beth said tentatively.

"These children don't need a caretaker," Mr. Gardiner growled. He winced at a metallic screech from the kitchen. "They need a cage and a lion tamer. I've seen better behaved wildcats."

In corroboration came more thuds and an outraged yelp from Millie.

"What do you know about children?" Mr. Gardiner looked her up and down like a farmer sizing up a skinny horse. "You're not much older than one yourself."

Beth drew herself up as tall as her petite stature allowed. "I am twenty-three years old, graduate of an excellent normal school, and a teacher for the past two years. I have been in charge of up to twenty-four children. Under my tutelage, these children never injured each other or committed serious property damage." She thought that detail important, given the apparent

70

potential for destruction from the two in this household. Trying to sound no less authoritative, she added a statement with less foundation in fact: "I'm also a widow, recently arrived from Seattle, and have a baby of my own."

Mr. Gardiner frowned at the sound of an unidentifiable crunch in the kitchen. "What's your name?"

"Annie Thompson." She had repeated the name often enough now that it no longer clumped in her mouth like an oversized wad of gum.

Then came a sudden howl, as if a child had just suffered mortal injury. Beth's experienced ears knew better; she could tell temper tantrum from pain. She suspected Mr. Gardiner could, too.

He nodded grimly. "Very well, Annie Thompson, you have a job. And I wish you good luck. You're going to need it."

The report and a first bill from Blacketer reached Guy's desk shortly after his return from a week at the meat-packing plant in Iowa. He wasn't surprised that Nat had routed it to him, arrogantly forcing his involvement in the search for Bethany Curtis in spite of his objection to it.

This *might* be an unfair suspicion, he granted reluctantly as he unfolded the report. Nat had other problems at the moment. The union issue at the meat-packing plant was heating up. Guy had collected the names of the ringleaders agitating for union organization, and Nat was exerting behind-the-scenes pressure to get rid of them.

The report was remote and impersonal. It didn't even refer to Bethany by name. The "subject," as if she were some inanimate object, was believed to have left Ft. Worth and the investigation was now centered in the Chicago area. The detective,

Guy thought wryly, had apparently been more successful than he had in extracting information from the boarding-house landlady. The bill was large, covering the services of several investigators by the agency.

But Chicago was a huge area, one in which even a young woman with spectacular auburn hair and a sweet baby might blend into anonymity.

Smart move, Bethany, he thought approvingly. In spite of the way she'd outwitted him and made him look like an incompetent fool, he hoped she'd make her escape work. *Keep 'em running in circles!*

Six

❧

"Come in."

The blond twins entered Beth's room giggling. After some seven weeks under her tutelage, Adrian and Ariana—such elegant names, Beth often thought, for such mischievous children!—were not models of decorum. They still delighted in tormenting poor Millie. But they had learned a few rules of good behavior, one of which was that they did not barge into Beth's room without knocking.

Beth lifted her brush from the painting of Joey she'd just started. She'd done one of the twins that had so pleased Mr. Gardiner that it was now at a professional art shop for framing. "And what are you two up to?" she inquired.

"Nothing, Miss Annie," Ariana said with an innocence that might or might not be genuine. She pursed her small lips as she studied the painting, like some miniature art critic. "C'n we paint, too?"

As a special treat, Beth sometimes let the twins smear paint on an old canvas. She'd found it released their creative energy in a way less objectionable than their former habit of gleefully crayoning the walls.

"Not tonight, because I'm leaving for midweek services at the church in a few minutes. But, if you're nice to Millie while I'm gone, you can both paint tomorrow."

Beth had Wednesday evening and Sunday off, although she spent half of Sunday with the twins anyway, taking them to church with her. She had continued to attend the friendly church to which Mrs. Welsch had introduced her, even though it was a considerable distance from the Gardiner house. The long walk had the unexpected benefit of discharging some of the twins' exuberant energy before arrival there, although those first Sundays with the twins had been daunting experiences indeed. Beth never had been able to figure out how Adrian got to church with a lizard in his pocket. Or how Ariana had managed to *take* a dime from the offering plate rather than give the coin she had brought to put in. And then there were the times when they got restless, and resorted to the tactics that worked with their mother, first whining and poking each other and then screaming their heads off!

But they were much better behaved these days, no longer given to screaming tantrums or physical attacks with flailing fists or butting heads. They had learned that when Beth said something she meant it, that there wouldn't be repetitious, meaningless pleas or threats or candy and ice cream bribes. Once they encountered no-nonsense authority that was consistent, firm, and fair, their basically bright and lovable natures came to the forefront.

Which didn't mean, unfortunately, that they were above doing something such as appropriating their mother's latest copy of *Vogue* and making paper airplanes and spitwads of the pages. Or brightly using Beth's insistence on truthfulness to inform a guest, when they were briefly brought down for showing off at one of Gillian's dinner parties, that he smelled like "stinky cigars."

"But you may walk Joey around the room, while I comb my hair," Beth now offered. The twins were surprisingly affectionate with Joey, and they loved to put him between them so he could take delighted steps with his chubby legs. He couldn't walk alone yet, but Beth knew it wouldn't be long now.

Beth kept an eye on the giggly threesome while she brushed her hair into a sleek auburn cap. It still looked too boyish to suit her, but at least strange stubs didn't stick out at odd angles. Afterward, the twins helped her take Joey downstairs and put him in the secondhand baby buggy she'd bought.

On the way to church, Beth alternated between a leisurely stroll and exuberant, unladylike dashes to give Joey the bouncy ride he loved. She felt carefree and happy here with the soft, early-evening dusk around her and the odd hump of Camelback Mountain a dark silhouette off to the northeast. She didn't consider herself and Joey totally safe from the Wilkersons, but neither was the danger of being found a gnawing worry these days. She was arranging Joey's blankets into a comfortable nest on the pew when Mrs. Welsch paused to whisper in her ear.

"Don't rush off after the service. I have to talk to you."

"Is something wrong?" Beth asked.

"I have to talk to you," Mrs. Welsch repeated more urgently. Her gaze skipped to the door as if she were apprehensively watching for someone. "It's very important."

Beth loved this midweek service of thoughtful study and prayer; only a small group of the faithful came and often they got deep into the Word. But tonight she had difficulty concentrating on the lesson as she uneasily wondered what was troubling Mrs. Welsch. It wasn't necessarily anything to do with her and Joey, she assured herself. Perhaps Mrs. Welsch just needed help composing another letter to the water department, against which she had an ongoing disagreement.

But that wouldn't account for the way Mrs. Welsch kept glancing at the door with worry lines cutting deeply into her face.

After the final hymn, Beth asked Mrs. Welsch if she'd like to walk over to the little diner a few blocks away so they could have a cup of coffee while they talked.

Another furtive glance at the door. "No. I don't think we should be seen together."

The alarm she'd been holding back jolted through Beth. "What do you mean?"

"A friend who rents rooms mentioned a couple of days ago that a man had come around looking for a young woman and baby. Today he came to see *me*. He said he was looking for his sister, who had disappeared after a family disagreement. He said their father was very ill and desperately wants to see her and the baby again before it's too late. And also that she has a large inheritance coming if he can find her."

Guy! Making up some tear-jerker story to induce coopera-tion in his search for her, because the blunt truth, *We want to find her so we can steal her baby,* wouldn't win them much sym-pathy or assistance. And, with his usual preoccupation with money, he'd added a phony inheritance, too!

Guy had been in Beth's thoughts numerous times these past weeks, thoughts usually accompanied by uneasy apprehension. But a time or two she'd wondered what sort of man he'd have become if, like Sylvia, he'd held firm to his Christian faith. Would he still be the family "troubleshooter," living in the St. Louis mansion, driving his sleek new Packard? Or would his life have taken a different course entirely? In spite of the Wilkerson wealth and power, he hadn't struck her as a very happy or satisfied man.

"Then he described the woman and baby. Annie, he described *you*. You and Joey. He said you had beautiful auburn hair, that it used to go clear to your waist although it was probably short now."

"What did you tell him?"

Mrs. Welsch twisted her hands in guilty agitation. "I said you had stayed at my place for a few days. I thought it was so wonderful for you and Joey. An inheritance!"

Beth reached for the back of the pew to steady herself. She couldn't go back to the Gardiners, she thought in a wildfire of panic. Guy was probably there right now, waiting to confront her…or simply to snatch Joey.

"I was just about to tell him you were at the Gardiners, and then I got this prickly, shivery feeling at the back of my neck. Angel fingers, my mother used to call it. So I took another look at him, and I saw…well, *not* a loving brother looking for his lost sister."

Beth closed her eyes briefly. A prickle at the back of Mrs. Welsch's sinewy neck. *Thank you, Lord.*

"So then I decided that before I told him anything more I'd talk to you, and I just said I'd see what I could find out. He's coming back tomorrow afternoon." She peered at Beth anxiously. "I didn't want to run him off for good, just in case he really is your brother."

Beth squeezed Mrs. Welsch's arm gratefully. "Thank you. The only brother I have is dead, this man is no relation to me, and there's no inheritance. I can't explain it all now, but this man is a…a terrible danger and threat to Joey and me."

"I knew it! I knew he was up to no good, smiling and acting so friendly and concerned, and all the time his eyes were calculating and mean, like Judas Iscariot's eyes must have been when he was bargaining for thirty pieces of silver to betray Jesus. He even offered to pay *me* for information."

"This was a tall man, late twenties, with dark gold hair and silvery-gray eyes, a very good-looking and well-dressed man?"

Mrs. Welsch shook her head. "No. He was about forty. Medium height, heavy in the belly. Dark hair, going bald."

Beth's taut shoulders slumped in relief. That definitely was not Guy! But then she realized all this meant was that they had put someone else on her trail, someone who, if he was systematically contacting every rooming house in town, was making a no-stone-unturned search for her. She remembered Guy's warnings about what his father was capable of and felt an icy prickle of fear.

Her mind squirreled through devious tunnels and chased down dead ends as she tried to figure out what to do. She should have had a plan already in place, she thought wildly, just in case something like this happened. Oh, she'd been so foolish to get complacent!

"Annie, you haven't done anything bad, have you?" Mrs. Welsch asked with a worried wrinkle of sun-weathered brow.

Beth gave her a reassuring hug. "No. Actually, it isn't me they want at all. It's Joey. I'm probably quite...disposable to them."

"Oh, Annie! And now they know you *are* here in Phoenix because I told them."

"But you can help throw them off my trail."

"How can I help?"

A pang of sorrow filled Beth's heart. She despised the lies she'd had to tell. And now she had to ask her friend to lie on her behalf...on Joey's behalf. It was all for Joey. And there was no other way.

Mrs. Welch touched her hand, as if sensing her discomfort. "Tell me, Beth. What can I do to help?"

Beth drew in a deep breath. "When this man comes back, tell him no one has seen me for several weeks, and I've probably gone to San Francisco because you'd overheard me asking about train schedules to there. Tell him you think I left with a man I'd been seeing here. And tell him I dyed my hair dark brown. Anything to send them off on a wild-goose chase with mistaken information." She hesitated. "I hate asking you to do this...to lie for me. It's just that Joey is in great danger. There's no other way."

"It's all right, Beth. I'll do whatever's necessary."

"There's something else." She swallowed. "Demand money before you tell them anything."

"Demand money!" Mrs. Welsch gasped, taken aback.

"These people believe money can buy anything. They're more apt to believe information they have to pay for." Mrs. Welsch looked so stricken that Beth shook her head helplessly.

"I'll tell him whatever I have to, to protect you and Joey," Mrs. Welsch said stoutly. Her gaze flicked apprehensively toward the door again. "But I think the man may have followed me here tonight."

"Here?" Beth repeated in dismay. Her mind whipped through a maze of dead ends before settling on a plan. "Okay, you stay here in the church as long as you can. As long as the baby buggy is outside, this man, if he's watching, should assume Joey and I are still in here too. I'll sneak out the back way and take a roundabout route home."

"Carrying the baby all that way?"

"I'll manage. I'll get the buggy later." Unless the Wilkersons got her first.

Beth finished bundling Joey in his blanket, slipped through the kitchen and out the back door. She wanted to peer around front to see if someone was watching, but she resolutely curbed that dangerous curiosity and hurried down the alley, grateful for a screen of picket fence and shrubs. At the street, rather than take a visible sidewalk route, she dashed across to another alley. Down two more alleys, and then, head ducked low over Joey, a furtive cut across several yards to a different street. *Guide me, Lord, please!*

Headlights suddenly targeted her, and she flung herself and Joey headlong into the shadow of a tree, protectively curving her body around his small one. She felt a little foolish when the old Model T merely stopped at the next house and a tired workingman got out and went to his door.

Joey whimpered as she walked and ran and stumbled, picked herself up and ran again. Her shoulders and back ached with the weight of him in her arms, but she didn't pause to rest until sharp stitches stabbed her side and stole her breath and she could go no farther.

She sank to the sandy ground, heart pounding, lungs burning, legs rubbery, dizzy stars whirling behind her eyes. She felt as if she had been running forever.

And this, she thought bleakly, was only the beginning.

$\mathscr{S}even$

G uy smiled as he read the first paragraph of Blacketer's report. After weeks of searching, the detective agency had been unable to find any trace of Bethany in the Chicago area and now doubted she had ever been there. She'd sent them on a wild-goose chase. Good for her!

During the last few weeks, thinking often about his dead sister and Bethany and the baby, he'd become even more convinced that Joseph should remain with Bethany. A half-remembered Bible verse about training a child in the way he should go kept running through his mind. He'd felt an odd desire to study the full verse, and, after digging through old boxes in his closet, finally located a Bible Mrs. Sommersby had given him years ago. He had no idea where the verse was located, however, and couldn't find it even after several frustrating searches. He couldn't understand why finding this verse suddenly seemed so important. It was, in fact, a rather annoying compulsion.

The report continued in the detective's usual stilted style, a style that Blacketer apparently felt elevated his sleazy work to a more dignified level. The report was written on plain paper, only the word CONFIDENTIAL stretched across the top.

Beneath the heading were the words, "Further intensive investigation in Ft. Worth revealed that subject departed that area in disguise and is now hiding somewhere in the Phoenix, Arizona, area. Exact whereabouts should be identified within the next few days."

The mention of Bethany in disguise intrigued and delighted Guy. No wonder, when he was looking for her, she had vanished as if whisked away by an angel!

His smile evaporated as he reread the report. Even though Bethany had managed to muddy her trail temporarily, bulldog Blacketer was closing in now. He shoved the report aside when the phone rang and his father's secretary told him Nat wanted to see him immediately. With his mind on Bethany, Guy entered his father's office expecting the search for her was also on his father's mind, but Nat's concerns at the moment were elsewhere.

"We've got big trouble at the meat-packing plant," Nat said without preliminaries. The diamond stickpin in his tie flashed a brilliant dazzle. Nat generally frowned on flamboyance, but he liked an occasional discreet touch of wealth to emphasize his status. "The union organizers are getting stronger and bolder every day."

Guy wasn't surprised. During the week he'd spent hanging around the Iowa plant pretending to be a down-and-outer looking for work, he'd felt a potential for explosion simmering like dynamite stew.

"You can't blame the workers for wanting more money. Wages are down to a third of what they were a few years ago." He'd been shocked to realize that he'd spent more on a new cashmere overcoat than those hard-working men earned in two months.

"Not my fault times are tough," Nat growled. "They're lucky to have any jobs at all."

"But it probably wouldn't take more than a couple of dollars a week per man to settle them down," Guy argued. The meat-packing plant had been making money even in these depression times. "It's hard, dirty, dangerous work. I saw a man get half his hand sliced off by a meat saw."

"If you give in to 'em once, they'll suck you dry."

"There's talk that Roosevelt will try to get minimum wage laws passed soon, and then we'll have to give raises anyway."

The "bank holiday" the new president, Franklin Delano Roosevelt, had declared soon after his inauguration had ended a few days ago, and everyone was expecting further bold action to lift the nation out of depression. Nat dismissed Roosevelt with a contemptuous flip of his hand.

"I'm not giving them another nickel," he said stubbornly.

"So what do you have in mind?"

They'd already offered "financial incentives" to the biggest union agitators, actually bribes disguised as attractive business deals, but the men hadn't succumbed to the lure. Nor had they given in when a corporation Nat had set up acquired the mortgages on their homes and threatened foreclosure.

"It's time for action, the only kind of action men like this understand."

Guy tapped his fingers on his thigh. Confrontation. Violence. There had been violence in various industries around the nation during strikes or when workers were fired and replaced with others desperate enough to work for any wage. Nat already had thug-tough security guards at the meat-packing plant. "If there's a confrontation, things could get ugly fast," Guy warned.

"There isn't going to be confrontation at the plant. We don't need a bunch of hotheads wrecking the place." Nat opened a drawer and drew out the list of names Guy had compiled during his week of undercover investigation at the plant. Attached were notes, maps, and schematic drawings. "What we do now is teach a couple of these troublemakers a lesson."

As if he were merely structuring some new financial venture, Nat briskly outlined his plan. Guy listened with appalled disbelief.

Guy knew Nat went after what he wanted; he knew Nat didn't let legal restrictions or ethics stand in his way. Usually Nat relied on clever financial manipulations to reach his goals or punish his enemies, although Guy knew that hired goons had occasionally carried the action into the physical arena of muggings or "accidents." Yet this scheme to teach the union organizers a warning lesson went beyond anything Guy could have imagined.

"Wait a minute," Guy cut in as Nat got down to a discussion of combustible materials. "You're talking about torching these men's homes?"

"That ought to get the message across. Make trouble at Wilkerson Meat Packing, and you pay."

Guy jumped to his feet. "You can't do this! This is arson. It might even be murder! These men have families. Children could be trapped inside those burning buildings."

Nat merely shrugged.

"You don't care if they don't get out?" Guy stared at his father, seeing a well-dressed, middle-aged businessman who exuded solid, conservative respectability. A man who, under all that, was calmly planning arson and possible murder. "What if it were *your* grandson trapped in some deliberately set inferno?"

"My grandson has nothing to do with this!" Nat snapped angrily, as if Guy had invaded some untouchable sanctuary. "Leave him out of it."

Guy took a steadying breath. Okay, wrong line of attack. Appealing to Nat's conscience was a waste of time. "Look at it this way, then. What if whoever you hire to do this gets caught? You think they won't squeal their heads off and implicate us?"

"I have no intention of hiring some outsider to carry out a mission this delicate. I assume that you—just as I was when on a similar mission at your age—are clever enough *not* to get caught."

The implication of Nat's words snagged on the surface of Guy's comprehension, then plunged deep. "You want *me* to sneak out there and torch two homes?" The further realization that Nat had at some time done something similar hit Guy like a rabbit punch from behind.

"You sound shocked."

"I can't believe you'd think I could do this."

"That hotel manager you fired down in Florida last year? I understand he committed suicide two months later."

Guy's clenched fists suddenly felt numb. He hadn't known that.

"The information you turned up about that foreman who was sneaking products out of the mill on the sly? Seems he had an unfortunate encounter with a street thug and got his right hand smashed."

Guy knew his "troubleshooting" activities had been rough on some people, obviously rougher in some instances than he'd ever realized. But he'd always felt his actions were justified because they concerned company disloyalty or cheating, all of which he disliked as much as Nat did. But *this*…

"I won't do it," he stated flatly. He planted his knuckles on the desk, his eyes locked with Nat's. *"I will not do it."*

"There's a generous bonus in it for you."

If enough money is involved, almost anything is for sale. His own words to Bethany shot out of nowhere to confront him. Nat obviously assumed *he* was for sale. He always had been before this.

"No."

"There is no place in this organization for those who put squeamishness or fear above family interests." Nat's voice remained calm, but his anger at Guy's defiance blazed in the steel flash of his eyes.

"Fear?" No, he wasn't *afraid* to do what Nat asked, and he didn't doubt he could complete the task successfully; it was simply that it went far beyond what he could do and live with himself. He shook his head in contemptuous dismissal of his father's taunts.

Then he repeated that other, more relevant word with sudden loathing. "Family? You have no idea what the real meaning of *family* is. To you it's control, everyone bending to your will, and you rip out whatever and whoever conflicts with that iron will. Even Sylvia."

Guy stopped when he came to his beloved sister's name. She had done, he realized slowly as his eyes remained locked with his father's, what he should also have done a long time ago. What he should have done when he realized Nat did not intend to discontinue his relentless stalking of Bethany and Joseph.

"I'm getting out," he said. He straightened, the expensive desk beneath his hands suddenly feeling invisibly stained and repulsive.

"What do you mean, 'getting out'?" Nat scoffed.

"Out. Out of anything to do with Wilkerson businesses. Out of the mansion. Out."

"You're talking like a fool—"

"I've *been* a fool."

"You're soft, Guy. Soft and weak." Nat's voice was soft and menacing. "I should have known you'd never amount to anything when you went along with Sylvia on that religious hayride."

Guy did not remind his father that he'd been off that "hayride" for years now. Was abandoning that Christian faith another of the mistakes he'd made in his life? "I'll be out of my office within an hour."

"That's your final decision?" Nat asked, and Guy heard an interior echo of similar words he'd said to Bethany.

He started to reply, as Bethany had, *Yes, that's my final decision.* Instead he leaned over Nat's desk until his eyes were inches from his father's. "No, *this* is my final decision." He stared unflinchingly at the man in front of him. "If I hear of any 'accident' to anyone connected with the meat-packing plant, by fire or otherwise, or if any children are injured or killed, I will make certain the police know exactly where the trail of guilt begins."

"Walk out and you can never expect anything more from me," Nat snarled, backing away. "Not while I'm alive. Not ever."

Guy cut him off. "The last thing I want is anything more from you, alive or dead."

He stormed back to his office, but after a cold glance around the room he knew he didn't need an hour to get out. There was nothing here he wanted. He grabbed his coat and hat.

Then he paused as his gaze fell on the report from Blacketer. On sudden angry impulse he ripped the paper to shreds and rained the tattered bits into the wastebasket.

A lot of good that did, he thought wryly as he watched the shreds flutter to the bottom of the basket. There'd simply be another report when Blacketer found Bethany, which apparently could be very soon now. He shuddered at the thought of baby Joseph being "rescued" and trapped here under Nat's ruthless thumb.

Unless...

He yanked a piece of paper out of the bottom drawer of his

desk and slipped it into the typewriter on a stand in the corner of his office. Standing at the machine he carefully typed a single word, CONFIDENTIAL, at the top of the page. Below it he rapidly composed a few lines in Blacketer's stilted style:

"Further intensive investigation in the Chicago area has revealed that subject departed that city in disguise and is now hiding in some unknown location outside the boundaries of the forty-eight states. As subject is now out of reach, we regretfully advise that nothing is to be gained by further search and have concluded our investigation."

Guy folded the sheet and tucked it in a plain envelope on which he typed Nat's name and office address, adding in capital letters off to the side: CONFIDENTIAL. TO BE OPENED BY ADDRESSEE ONLY. He plastered a stamp in the corner and slipped the envelope into his coat pocket.

One more chore.

Blacketer sounded surprised when Guy informed him over the telephone that the agency was to contact their investigator in Phoenix and instruct him to discontinue the search immediately.

"*Immediately,*" Guy repeated to emphasize that point. "We are no longer interested in locating this subject."

"Okay, got it." Blacketer sounded as if he were speaking with a cigar hanging out the side of his mouth, his slangy tone at odds with the stilted wording of his reports. "I'll send a wire right away."

Three hours later, the loaded Packard stood at the side door of the stone mansion like some shimmering magic chariot, trunk strapped on the rear, afternoon sun shooting a silvery flash off the gleaming hood ornament. He'd already mailed the letter and cleaned out his checking account. He'd had to leave a good many belongings behind, of course. But how many pairs of Italian leather shoes did a man really need?

He started the engine, but instead of putting the car in gear, he just sat there as an odd feeling unexpectedly rolled over him. A strange feeling of…what? Being, as the old saying went, all dressed up and nowhere to go? No, it was an unfamiliar and unlikely feeling of being untethered, adrift. Lost.

Was this how Bethany had felt as she fled in the night?

No, her situation was far more desperate, he thought guiltily, because she'd had him on her heels. Plus the responsibility of a baby. But she'd had one thing he didn't have, he conceded: a faith and trust in God to guide her.

What did he have? An expensive education. An expensive car. A carload of expensive clothes and possessions. A well-filled wallet.

And a peculiar feeling that Bethany was better equipped to handle the unknown than he was.

He tossed away the disquieting feeling. He wasn't lost; he was simply free to go anywhere, do anything.

He'd long wanted to get into newspaper work. What better time than right now? He'd go to some big city with a hard-hitting urban newspaper. New York. Chicago. Los Angeles.

But a different destination came to mind.

He immediately rejected it. Foolish. Illogical. A city…a state…in the middle of nowhere. A place he had never seen, or ever felt any burning desire to see. Did it even have a newspaper? For all he knew, they were still in the horse and buggy days out there. But it was a city that now had a magnetic appeal all its own.

He suddenly smiled, then put the Packard into gear and pulled onto the road.

Eight

✍

A nnie!"
Beth rolled her eyes as the yell floated up from the floor
below. Gillian had come home from the newspaper office
early today because she was giving a dinner party, and this was
at least the third time she had yelled for Beth. Beth didn't consider herself Gillian's servant, but apparently that was an opinion not shared by Gillian. Beth often found herself rinsing out
silk stockings or pressing a garment or replacing a button.

"You two may take a recess and play with your new train,"
Beth instructed the twins. They were in the big attic room that
served as both playroom and schoolroom for the children. Joey
was napping in Beth's bedroom. "When I get back we'll look
out the window and see how many things we can name that
start with a 'sh' sound."

Adrian raced for the play train, but Ariana dashed to the
window. She loved word games and could already read better
than many third-graders Beth had taught.

Beth descended the steep stairs and stopped at the doorway
of Gillian's dazzling white and gold bedroom, complete with
white radio and telephone. "You called?" Beth said, squelching

an impulse toward saying, more accurately, *You yelled, screeched, shrieked?*

Gillian was frowning at a slink of black velvet on a satin hanger. "The hook is loose here at the waist," she fretted. "Can you fix it?"

"I thought you were planning to wear the emerald silk." Just this morning, Gillian had demanded that it be pressed.

"Oh, I was, but it's just too fussy and unsophisticated. I really need something new, of course, but the goods in the stores here are so terribly provincial."

Beth ignored this petulant complaint. "Will you want the children brought down this evening?"

Gillian never let the twins eat with guests at her dinner parties, but, now that their wildcat behavior was somewhat tamed, Mr. Gardiner liked to show them off before dinner.

Beth waited while Gillian tapped her wine-red lower lip with a glossy nail of matching color. She knew that Gillian had arranged this small dinner party specifically so she could invite a new reporter at the newspaper. A mere reporter seemed an unlikely target for Gillian's interest, but this one apparently had something special that attracted her.

"I suppose Father will insist on it," Gillian finally decided grudgingly. "Dress Ariana in the pink organdy, and Adrian in that darling black suit I bought him. And a bow tie."

Ariana enjoyed dressing up, and she pirouetted in the frilly dress like a twirling petal; but getting Adrian into a little white shirt, the hated "darling black suit," and a bow tie was like trying to dress a small, rigid statue. He didn't fight, but neither did he cooperate.

Gillian paused in the twins' room on her way downstairs to

greet the first guests. She was spectacularly eye-catching in the black velvet dress that molded her slim waist and bared her back, her hair styled in a copy of moviestar Marlene Dietrich's elegant waves. Her lips were dramatic red, her eyebrows symmetrical dark arches. Even Adrian relaxed his wooden stiffness to stare at her.

"Bring the children down in exactly fifteen minutes," Gillian instructed. She frowned at Beth's new green dress with a crisp white yoke, neither as sophisticated or daring as her own gown, but definitely fashionable and flattering. Gillian had mentioned before that Beth really should wear a uniform to suit her position, and Beth strongly suspected she was going to have some ugly and institutional-looking thing thrust on her any day now. "But don't stay more than ten minutes," Gillian added regally before turning on a slim heel and disappearing down the stairs.

Sounds of chiming doorbell, laughter, and murmurs of social small talk drifted up from below as Beth brushed her hair after dressing Adrian. She was ready to take the twins down to present them to the guests when she discovered that Adrian was strangely shoeless.

"My shoes acciden'ly fell downstairs," he muttered rebelliously.

Beth doubted the accidental nature of such a fall, but she'd deal with that later. Leaning over the railing, she spotted the shoes near the door between the foyer and living room and dashed downstairs to retrieve them. Her gaze briefly flicked over the dozen or so guests as she passed the open door to the living room.

Gillian stood out like some exotic black orchid among the more conservatively attired guests, her red nails flashing as she talked vivaciously with a tall man with dark gold hair leaning casually against the fireplace. This must be her targeted reporter, Beth decided. The identification was confirmed when the tinkling of Gillian's laughter carried toward her. Gillian flirtatiously tilted her head to one side.

And Beth saw his face.

She stopped, frozen, the small shoes dangling limply from her outstretched hand. No, it couldn't be. Impossible.

She stared only a shocked moment, then whirled and dashed up the stairs, landing in her bedroom with shoulders heaving. She leaned against the closed door as if an armed predator were hard on her heels, eyes also closed as she tried to compose herself. Surely she was mistaken.

Yes, this man had dark gold hair streaked with bronze. Yes, he was tall and ruggedly built and suavely dressed. Yes, he had angular, aristocratic cheekbones and an elegantly casual stance.

Yes, he looked like Guy Wilkerson.

But that didn't mean he *was* Guy Wilkerson! Guy was a troubleshooter for the family empire back in St. Louis, not a newspaper reporter here in Phoenix…wasn't he?

It had been almost a month now since the scare when the man had come to Mrs. Welsch seeking the whereabouts of an auburn-haired young woman and a baby. Beth had run home that night planning to toss everything into a suitcase and flee again. But heart-pounding reflection had warned her that if the Wilkersons were conducting this comprehensive a search for her, the railway and bus stations could also be under surveillance. So she had decided to conceal herself at the Gardiners for a few more days while Mrs. Welsch tried to throw the investigator off the trail with misinformation, and while *she* tried to think of some untraceable means of escape.

For several days she had jumped nervously whenever telephone or doorbell rang; she made excuses to stay hidden inside the house, not even going out for church; she never got more than a few feet from Joey, fearful he might somehow be snatched from under her nose.

But the man had not returned to interrogate or bribe Mrs. Welsch, not the following day nor any day since. No strangers had come around the Gardiner house asking nosy questions; no unfamiliar cars prowled the neighborhood. Everything was calm and normal.

A week later, venturing out at the unlikely hour of daybreak, Beth cautiously retrieved the baby buggy from where Mrs. Welsch had shoved it behind the church.

By two weeks, Beth's nerves had stopped crackling like static electricity under her skin, and she could almost believe the whole thing had been an innocent error. Perhaps the man really had been looking for a lost sister and had never returned to Mrs. Welsch's because he'd found her elsewhere.

But now that comforting theory was in chaos, because Guy Wilkerson was right here in this very house!

She paced to the window and looked for a sleek silver Packard among the automobiles lined up on the street, but moonlight shining through the elm and ash trees dappled the cars with camouflaging shadows. No, it couldn't be him, she argued, reversing her stand of only a moment ago. Her nerves had imagined him, given his face to some other tall, ruggedly built man with gold-bronze hair.

Beth jumped when a knock rattled the door, suddenly aware she had been standing there in the dark for...how long?...with Adrian's small shoes clutched in her hand.

"Annie, are you in there?" Gillian, unlike the twins, impatiently shoved the door open without waiting for a response. "Whatever are you doing here in the dark? The children should have been brought down five minutes ago."

"I'm…not feeling well." Certainly the truth, Beth thought, considering the Ferris-wheel whirl in her stomach. "Perhaps I could finish dressing Adrian and you could take the children down yourself."

Gillian was not interested in Beth's inconvenient physical complaints. "I cannot entertain guests and see to the children as well," she snapped. "Bring them down immediately."

Gillian departed, leaving the door open, and Beth took a steadying breath. She was behaving foolishly, she chastised herself, like some wide-eyed child imagining ghosts or monsters just because the floor creaked. She forced herself to return to the twins' room, put Adrian's shoes on his uncooperative feet and give Ariana's curls another swish with a brush.

That was *not* actually Guy Wilkerson down there, she assured herself once more. But just in case…

"Wait here," she instructed the twins at the head of the stairs.

She dashed back to her own room and flicked on the lamp, pausing to give Joey a reassuring kiss when he half-woke. In the bottom of the nightstand drawer she found what she was looking for. She slammed the glasses on her face and pulled her short hair forward, covering her temples and forehead almost to the heavy rims. She looked, she thought wildly as she peered in the mirror, like some strange creature out of a comic strip.

Which was fine, just so long as she looked nothing like Bethany Curtis of Ryman Springs, Oklahoma.

A hand gripping each child, she led them downstairs to join the guests. The distorting glasses made her feel a little dizzy and disoriented, and she held her head unnaturally high to keep from stumbling over her feet. Gillian hurried over, all smiles, and knelt down to put an arm around each child.

"And here are my little darlings," she cooed. "Annie, dear,

do they have something planned for us tonight?"

"Ariana has a little poem to recite."

While Ariana recited the poem, Beth surreptitiously scanned the room for the man who looked like Guy Wilkerson. She was horrified to find him staring back at her and quickly averted her eyes.

Even with the dizzying distortion of the glasses, there was no mistaking Guy Wilkerson.

Her thoughts and emotions careened between panic and confusion. Why was he pretending to be a reporter? Did he recognize her? She desperately wanted to look at him again, but she forced herself to keep her eyes on Ariana. She must not let him catch any trace of recognition…or fear…on *her* face.

She intended to grab the twins and retreat immediately after the poem, but Ariana skipped over to her grandfather, plopped herself down on his knee, and started chattering vivaciously.

"Such lovely children," an older woman's voice on Beth's left said. "Such a wonderful time of life, when the children are at that age."

Beth turned to the woman in relief…anything to keep busy until she could escape! "Yes, that's so true." With further relief she saw out of the corner of her eye that Gillian was smiling up at Guy and had trapped his arm in the curl of her hand.

No…he was deftly removing the hand…excusing himself…and stalking straight as a tightrope walker toward Beth.

And it was *she* who was trapped, she realized wildly. Skewered. Impaled like a butterfly on a pin.

Guy was less than four feet from the auburn-haired woman when the little boy tugged on her hand and whispered something in her ear. He pointed to his feet, the woman looked surprised, and they both scooted toward the door. Guy followed but got hemmed in by a wide matron in a pink dress. By the time he reached the door all he saw was a pair of slim legs and trim ankles disappearing at the top of the stairs.

Frustrated, he just stood there in the doorway, his back to Gillian and the other guests. Was it her? This woman was about the same size and age as Bethany, the same slim, fine-boned figure, and the hair was the same flaming auburn. But with the heavy, dark-rimmed glasses and the short, peculiar hairstyle concealing her face....

Concealing. The significant word jumped at him out of his own thoughts. *Concealing.* As in disguise?

"Guy, whatever are you doing?" Gillian asked, coming up behind him. "You rushed off as if you thought I was going to bite you!" She half-smiled, half-pouted, a combination Guy did not find particularly attractive.

"The children's governess.... What's her name?" he asked bluntly.

Gillian looked annoyed but finally said, "Annie Thompson."

Which meant nothing, of course. It was highly unlikely Bethany would be using her real name.

"Has she been with you long?"

"Two or three months, I suppose."

A bit indefinite, but it fit into the time period of Bethany's disappearance.

"Do you know if she's local, or recently arrived from somewhere else?"

"I have *no* idea." Gillian tossed her dark hair, obviously miffed with all these questions that were not about her. "Father hired her."

"Will she be joining us for dinner?"

"Of course not. Servants don't dine with us." Gillian bristled as if appalled at the suggestion.

"It's just that—" Guy floundered for some logical but unrevealing reason to explain his interest. "—that she resembles someone I used to know."

"An old girlfriend?" Gillian's tone was teasing, but sparks of displeasure peppered her dark eyes.

Guy knew Gillian had invited him to this dinner because he hadn't responded to her flirty hints at the newspaper office that he should ask her out. That she did not appreciate what she considered an excessive interest in her children's governess was obvious. Aware that Gillian was his only source of information at the moment, a source that could dry up if he was not careful, he breezily laughed at the question.

"No, I prefer a more sophisticated type," he said with a meaningful smile and quirk of eyebrow.

That mollified her, and she gave him a silky smile. Her daughter ran up, but Gillian just gave the little girl a pat on the shoulder and told her to run upstairs with Annie and Adrian.

"It's just that some relatives had this marvelous nanny taking care of their son, and then she became…indisposed," he explained. "They wondered what had become of her." It was an awkward bit of manipulation of the truth, but not really an *untruth.*

"Annie seems healthy enough. She's always tromping halfway across town to go to church."

Bethany would "tromp" halfway across town to go to church!

One more vitally important question. "Does she have…" He paused. How would Bethany have identified Joseph? He knew how he, in her tenuous position, would have done it. "A child of her own?"

"Yes. She's a widow and has a baby, oh…less than a year

old." A dismissive wave of Gillian's red-nailed hand indicated such minor details were irrelevant to her.

Guy wanted to ask if the baby was boy or girl; he wanted to know a name! But just then dinner was announced, and he had to follow the other guests to the dining table, impatiently sit through roast beef and glazed carrots and listen to talk about everything from the repeal of Prohibition to the wonderful new Barrymore film.

Which didn't keep his thoughts away from the auburn-haired governess.

In spite of a lack of informational details and a considerable difference in appearance, he was almost certain this was Bethany. He could swear she'd stiffened with recognition when she saw him and that her exit had been unnecessarily hasty.

Because, seeing him, she must be terrified. Somehow he had to let her know he was no threat, that he had no intention of revealing her whereabouts to his father. He could simply ring her up and tell her, of course. Would she believe him? He wouldn't if he were her. She might suspect it was simply a trick to trap her, with the result that his attempt to reassure her would have the opposite effect of stampeding her into another desperate flight.

There was also the possibility that he was wrong, he conceded. Sometimes it came as a small shock to him to realize that he had actually spent less than one day of his life with Bethany; somehow he felt he knew her much better than that. Yet, in truth, he didn't really know her, and if this woman was not Bethany, he could easily create an awkward and embarrassing situation for both her and himself.

He could also be making a mistake, he had to admit, because he wanted this to be Bethany...and not solely because he wanted to reassure her that she was out of danger. Gillian's sharp-eyed suspicion that his interest in her children's gover-ness was too intense and too personal was not necessarily unwarranted.

It also seemed unlikely that after making a fairly determined effort to locate Bethany in the Phoenix area, including using the newspaper's resources, that he'd have the good luck simply to stumble across her by accident here. Although he remembered Mrs. Sommersby from long ago saying something about noth-ing happening by mere luck or chance, that all was God-directed.

Yet it seemed unlikely God would direct his way to Bethany, he thought wryly.

Obviously, the first thing to do, he decided as he ate his way through the creamy chocolate dessert without really tasting it, was somehow determine if this actually was Bethany. It was time, he thought with sudden inspiration, to count freckles!

With that goal in mind, he took Gillian's hands in his when she walked with him to the door later.

"It was a marvelous evening. Thanks for inviting me. I was wondering…Would you like to take a drive out in the country on Saturday?" The newspaper didn't publish on Sunday, so he usually had Saturday off. His "beat" was the courts and law enforcement offices, not the important, late-breaking news sto-ries. "I hear that the desert wildflowers are quite beautiful this time of year."

He doubted Gillian had any great interest in wildflowers; he suspected her shallow character bore an unfortunate resem-blance to his brother's social-climbing wife back in St. Louis. But a drive was the only activity he could think of that fit the scheme he had in mind.

"Why, yes, I'd love that!" Gillian agreed enthusiastically. "I'll have Millie make a picnic lunch for us."

Yes, even better than just a drive! "That sounds wonderful. Say, why don't you bring the twins along?" he added as if it were a casual afterthought.

"They can be a handful if cooped up for long. It wouldn't give us much chance to get to know each other better."

"Bring their governess along to watch them, then," he urged. "I'd really like a chance to get to know the children better, too."

Gillian ran a fidgety finger across his knuckles, obviously not eager to include this entourage. "She'd have to bring the baby," she demurred with a small frown ridging her smooth forehead.

"That's fine. There's plenty of room in the car for everyone." He tossed this out as if it were some magnanimous gesture on his part rather than the real target of his scheme. "I'll see you all about ten o'clock on Saturday, then, and we'll make a full day of it." He gave her hands a quick squeeze and left before she could think of some excuse that would thwart his clever plan to include the auburn-haired governess.

Outside, sitting in his car, he studied the single light glowing from a side window on the second floor of the Gardiner house. Bethany and baby Joseph's room? If she was Bethany...

Surely, during a day-long drive and picnic, he could figure that out for certain.

Nine

❧

Beth eyed the twins as they fidgeted by the picnic basket at the front door, Ariana in a starched white eyelet dress and Adrian in a stiff white shirt and cuffed pants. They were, in Beth's opinion, ridiculously overdressed for a desert picnic on a hot May day. She'd put little Joey in comfortable cotton rompers, and he was sitting on the floor making happy noises.

Beth wore her glasses and one of the blue and white striped uniforms Gillian had brought home the previous day. She couldn't be certain Gillian had picked the largest, dowdiest, and most unflattering garments she could find. But they certainly seemed suitable to take along as striped awnings for picnic shade, she thought wryly.

"Now, do we have everything?" Gillian fussed. She looked fresh and lovely in flowing white trousers and silky blouse trimmed with jet buttons. In frivolous high-heeled sandals, she apparently did not intend any on-foot exploration of the desert.

"Wouldn't the children enjoy the picnic more if they were dressed in something comfortable?" Beth felt sorry for them, trapped in their fussy little outfits.

"I want Guy to see us as sophisticated and urbane, people of good taste and breeding and culture. I don't want the children looking like grubby little ragamuffins. Guy is not exactly what he appears to be," Gillian added with a significant nod.

Gillian's observation somehow alarmed Beth. "Oh?"

"I don't know why he's pretending to be merely a common reporter, although I do find it rather *intriguing*. Actually, he's from one of St. Louis's most distinguished and wealthy families. I doubt he plans to remain an underpaid reporter for long."

Beth had a good idea what Guy was doing; he was plotting to get Joey away from her. But why he'd chosen this odd, circuitous approach was indeed puzzling. Her skin prickled with fresh alarm at a sudden new thought. She'd tried, without success, to get out of this picnic because of her simple apprehension about seeing Guy again. But was it possible that he was boldly planning, under guise of an innocent picnic, to snatch Joey this very day?

"What makes you think that about his background?" Beth asked.

"Oh, well, one who knows can tell the difference in a person's class simply by looking and listening," Gillian pointed out with a high-nosed superiority that suggested these differences were beyond someone of Beth's lower-bred origins. "Also, when he said he was from St. Louis, I telephoned a friend who lives there now and asked if she knew anything about a Wilkerson family, and she told me all about the Wilkersons' big textile mill and important social status."

Beth was surprised that Gillian was confiding all this to her, a mere governess, but apparently she was so pleased with her own cleverness that she couldn't keep it to herself. "How interesting," Beth murmured noncommittally.

"He's been a bit shy about approaching me, but a man isn't

interested in getting to know a woman's children unless he has serious intentions," Gillian proclaimed with confidence.

Shy was not a word Beth would ever have used to describe Guy. Although *shyster* might fit, she decided uneasily.

The doorbell rang, and Gillian motioned for Beth to get the door while she struck a glamour pose by the picnic basket. Beth nervously clumped her short hair around the disguising glasses. She'd escaped facing Guy head-on at the dinner party because of that last-minute discovery by Adrian that in her agitation she'd put his shoes on the wrong feet, but there was no escaping this confrontation.

They stared at each other when Beth opened the door, his silver-gray eyes and sharply defined jaw distorted into shimmery waves by Beth's glasses. But not so distorted but what she could see him studying her. When he moved his head forward as if trying to peer through her heavy glasses, she instinctively moved hers back.

"Mrs. Thompson, isn't it?" he finally said politely after the awkward pause. He was casually dressed in tan cotton pants and jaunty straw hat with a feather in the band. He looked handsome and carefree, the perfect picture of a young man arriving to take his best girl out for a country picnic.

The image briefly confused Beth, and she wondered why she found the idea of Guy being attracted to shallow, vain Gillian vaguely annoying and disappointing. But his romantic involvements were certainly no interest of hers, she assured herself firmly as she stepped aside without acknowledging his greeting.

Gillian swung forward with that hip-swaying walk Beth had seen her practice in front of a full-length mirror. "Guy! What a wonderful idea this is. The twins and I have so been looking forward to it."

He had a little doll for Ariana and a teddy bear for Adrian, but after giving the gifts to the twins he unexpectedly swooped Joey up in his strong hands. Beth's fear that he was brazenly planning to snatch the baby flared again.

She hefted the cloth bag which held Joey's and the twins' things, plus a book she'd borrowed from Mr. Gardiner's den. Try to get out the door with him, she warned Guy with a glare of silent ferocity, and you'll find yourself flattened with a three-pound copy of *Plants and Animals of the Desert*.

Guy made no abrupt move to run, however, and Joey was giggling delightedly with the rough masculine attention as Guy playfully lifted him high overhead. "And who is this?" Guy inquired.

"That's Mrs. Thompson's baby," Gillian said. As if it were some unfair burden inflicted on her she added, "I told you we'd have to bring him along."

"What's his name?"

Guy looked at Beth for an answer, but it was Gillian who impatiently cut in with, "Joey. Shall we be on our way now?"

Beth hurriedly removed Joey from Guy's grasp, embarrassed when her fingers momentarily tangled with his. She carefully did not meet his eyes even as they awkwardly disengaged their hands, but she had the uneasy feeling he was still studying her.

The feeling continued after they were all settled in the car. Beth was in back with the children, her position on the seat chosen before she realized it put her in line with Guy's reflection in the rearview mirror and afforded him an equal view of her. He had donned dark sunglasses, so she couldn't see his eyes. The feeling that he was watching her was so strong and disquieting that she finally made an excuse to change places with the twins. A switch that did not go unnoticed.

"Are you uncomfortable, Mrs. Thompson?" Guy inquired,

raising his voice above the conversational level with Gillian in the front seat.

"No, I'm fine."

"Is it too crowded back there?"

"No, we're all fine."

"Where are we going?" Gillian cut in with a glare at Beth over the seat even though it was not Beth who had initiated the conversation with Guy.

"I thought we'd drive out toward the Superstition Mountains," Guy laughed. "There's supposed to be a golden treasure out there somewhere. Maybe we'll find it."

Gillian had *her* eye, Beth suspected, on the St. Louis treasures of the "distinguished and wealthy" Wilkerson family.

They drove east out of town. Joey immediately fell asleep in the smooth-riding car, and the drive was sufficient novelty for the twins that they forgot to squabble. Beth got out her plant and animal book so she'd be able to identify whatever she saw on the desert, only to discover that with the wavy distortion of the glasses she couldn't read a word. Frustrated, she stuffed the book back in the bag and sneaked a peek at the back of Guy's head. His dark-gold hair now showed no signs of the doctor's barbering, but, cautiously lifting the glasses for a better view, she detected a thin streak of scar extending below the hairline.

He unexpectedly half-turned his head, catching her with the glasses raised. "I hope you're enjoying the drive, Mrs. Thompson."

Beth hastily grabbed a handkerchief from the pocket of her uniform and energetically pretended to scrub the glasses clean, as if that were the sole reason she had removed them. After that she concentrated her gaze on the scenery. The glasses, fortunately, were not so distorting on distant views.

Civilization was encroaching, but east of the small settlement of Mesa the desert looked little changed from what it must have been before the white man came. Everything was in colorful bloom now, from clumps of ankle-high cactuses sporting oversized fuchsia-colored blossoms to deep carpets of spiky blue flowers. Blooms like small scarlet flames tipped the graceful, whip-like cactuses, and crowns of blooms circled the tops of fat cactus plants shaped like barrels. There were forests of the tall, spread-armed cactuses that towered with serene dignity over the surprising profusion of plant life below, and here and there a single spectacular spire of creamy blossoms rose from a whorl of spiky leaves at its base. Oh, how Beth wished she could peek into the book and put a name to everything!

The Superstitions loomed ever larger as they drove east, the leading edge a massive jumble of reddish-brown cliffs rising starkly from the desert floor. Burnt by relentless desert sun and cut by ragged crevices, the towering cliffs and mountains behind them lived up to their name, a forbidding warning to anyone bold and foolish enough to challenge their mysteries.

"I don't exactly know where we're going," Guy admitted after they passed a fork in the road. "Anyone have any suggestions for where we should have our picnic?"

Gillian studied the desert landscape with wary distaste, as if her suggestion would be anywhere but here, but Beth was intrigued by everything she saw. Including an odd, long-tailed bird that instead of flying away simply ran down the road with astonishing speed.

"Why don't we just follow the bird?" Guy suggested in an unexpectedly playful tone when the odd creature turned off on a set of dim tracks leading toward the massive walls of stone. "That okay with you, Mrs. Thompson?" he called over his shoulder.

Beth stared at the back of his head as he steered the Packard onto the dim tracks winding across the sandy desert. He'd called her Mrs. Thompson several times, always very politely, but suddenly it struck her that his manner was almost *too* polite, that he was actually subtly mocking her with the phony name.

The tracks led to an unexpectedly pleasant spot for the picnic. A cluster of tiny-leafed, green-gold trees with smooth, green bark provided shade. Old ashes within a circle of rocks showed that people had camped here in the past. A rocky creek nearby wasn't flowing, but the rocks still held a few shallow pools of water. The twins were no more out of the car than they had their shoes off and were delightedly squealing and sloshing in the water. Gillian looked at Beth as if she thought Beth should do something about this ragamuffin-type behavior, but Beth just busied herself with laying out the picnic things.

Actually, she wouldn't mind splashing in that water herself! Without the breeze created by the moving car, the day was hot enough to bring instant rivulets of perspiration to Beth's face. Joey woke, and Guy helped him toddle from the car out to the blankets Beth had spread. There, to Beth's surprise, he took off Joey's little soft-soled shoes and soon had Joey splashing in the water, too. Seeing the two of them together, they looked so much like father and son that Beth felt a sharp jolt of alarm. If she could see the family resemblance so plainly, could Guy also see it?

She got another jolt when they were all seated on the blankets, ready to start eating. With the voluminous skirt covering her, Beth sat comfortably cross-legged, Joey on her lap. Gillian had her legs tucked to the side, obviously trying for a graceful image but managing to look awkward as a bent toothpick instead.

"Perhaps Mrs. Thompson would offer the blessing?" Guy suggested.

Gillian looked surprised. Prayer was not part of everyday meals in the Gardiner household, but she gave a nod to signify Beth should comply with Guy's request. Beth, even as she offered a brief thanks, had the uneasy feeling that this was some small test or trap Guy had set for her. He knew Bethany Curtis's Christian convictions; was he trying to determine if "Mrs. Thompson" shared them?

Immediately afterward, as Beth was filling plates for the twins, he added, "There's a verse in the Bible that keeps running through my head, something about bringing up a child in the way he should go. I've looked, but I've never been able to find it. Can you tell me where it is, Mrs. Thompson?"

For a moment Beth was tempted to deny knowledge of any such verse, certain he was simply adding to his collection of bits of evidence to use against her. Yet denying such knowledge seemed, in a small way, a denial of Christ, which was not something she could do. Reluctantly she said, "You'll find it in Proverbs. I don't remember the exact chapter. Perhaps the twenty-first or twenty-second, somewhere in there."

"Thank you." His smile was enigmatic, but to Beth's blurred gaze it seemed to hold a hint of satisfaction, as if he'd just proved a point.

Beth's personal idea of a picnic was fried chicken and potato salad, but Millie, under Gillian's instructions, had sent dainty cucumber sandwiches cut into crustless triangles, grated ham sandwiches rolled and tied with little pink ribbons, a tomato and salmon salad, pressed veal loaf, rose-cut radishes and fancy, bite-sized tea cakes. All to be eaten on fine china with wine in crystal glasses for Guy and Gillian, lemonade in tumblers for Beth and the children.

In spite of her uneasiness, Beth was amused to see Guy look at everything as if he longed for something big and man-sized he could sink his teeth into, but the brief amusement was cut short when he leaned over to pass a plate to her and she felt his eyes studying her again, like a scientist targeting a suspicious specimen.

"Sandwich, Mrs. Thompson?"

Don't do that! She wanted to shout at him. *Stop studying me!* But she couldn't yell that out, of course, so she simply accepted a sandwich and kept her face averted.

The food, in spite of its delicate fussiness, was quite delicious, and little Joey had a great time squishing and eating a rolled sandwich almost by himself. The twins giggled and slyly jiggled their slices of gelatinous veal loaf at each other, but Beth managed to keep their behavior more or less up to Gillian's "well-bred" standards.

Afterward Gillian said to Beth, "After you clean up the picnic things, why don't you take the children for a walk?"

It was phrased as a casual suggestion, but Beth knew a command when she heard one. Beth didn't object to the order to disappear so Gillian could be alone with Guy. She was, in fact, delighted with the excuse to get out of Guy's presence. She hurriedly packed everything away in the wicker basket, collected her book and settled Joey on her hip. The twins bounced around like small tornadoes only occasionally touching ground.

But instead of cooperating with Gillian's little scheme, Guy bounded to his feet. "I'll come along. Somewhere I heard you should never venture out on the desert without water. I'll bring a bottle."

"For goodness sakes, Guy, they aren't going far enough to need a supply of water," Gillian snapped.

Beth echoed the protest. "That's right. We're just going to—" She looked around and hastily chose a nearby destination. "—to walk over there and look at that big cactus with all the arms."

"I'll come along to make certain you don't lose your way, then. It would be easy to get turned around out here."

"That isn't necessary. If we're not back by the time you're ready to leave, just honk the car horn." Beth felt a little desperate in the trap of his persistence, and the last thing she wanted was to be alone with him without the safety barrier of Gillian's presence. She also desperately wanted an opportunity to take the dizzying glasses off; she'd never worn them this long, and the world was beginning to feel as if it were in a slow spin around her. "We can always find our way back when we hear the horn."

"Oh, but *I* want to see that cactus, too," Guy said with cheerful stubbornness. He gave her an innocent grin. "I'm very interested in plant and animal life of the desert."

Beth glanced at Gillian for help, but the other woman looked as frustrated as Beth felt. Guy was apparently determined to accompany Beth, and there didn't seem much either Beth or Gillian could do about it.

Gillian got to her feet and brushed at desert grit that had settled on her white trousers. "I suppose I may as well come along, too," she muttered in a sulky tone. Her dark glance at Beth suggested this was somehow all Beth's fault.

They started out on the faint trail of tire tracks across the desert, Gillian determinedly marching along in her high heels beside Guy. The twins whooped and shrieked as they dashed around in some new game of cowboys and Indians. Beth brought up the rear with Joey.

They hadn't gone more than two hundred feet when Gillian had to stop and dump sand out of her sandals. Another hundred feet and a high heel slipped sideways on a pebble. Another few feet and the other heel sank deep in the small hole of some unseen desert creature.

Beth hastily set Joey down so he could toddle a few feet by himself. She had to do something or she was going to burst into totally unacceptable laughter at the sight of Gillian standing there hot and fuming, lopsided as a vehicle with a flat tire.

"This is ridiculous," Gillian finally snapped. "I'm going back to the car before I break an ankle."

She looked at Guy, obviously expecting him to accompany her, but all he did was say solicitously, "Do be careful walking in those high heels."

Gillian's withering glance could have shriveled a grape to a raisin on the spot, but Guy merely smiled benignly. She stalked off, the furious dignity of her departure somewhat marred by the dark smudge shaped like a frown on the backside of her trousers. The twins unexpectedly chose to abandon the walk and race after her.

And here *she* was, Beth realized with a hot wave of dismay, exactly where she did not want to be: alone with Guy Wilkerson.

W ell, Mrs. Thompson, it looks as if it's just the two of us."

Guy smiled, a lazy white flash against tanned skin that Beth suspected she might have found quite heart-fluttering if it weren't coming from *him.* She again had the feeling he was subtly mocking her with his frequent emphasis on "Mrs. Thompson," although now that they were alone it almost sounded like playful teasing. As if they both knew she wasn't *really* "Mrs. Thompson" but were joined in a little conspiracy to pretend she was.

"I'll have to go back and look after the twins."

"Let Gillian do it. It will do her good to take responsibility for them herself once in a while."

Beth's sentiments exactly, although she was surprised to hear the opinion coming from Guy.

"I can carry the baby for you," Guy offered. "He's getting to be quite a heavy load now."

Beth's nerves quivered like a radio antenna twanged against hard metal. *Now,* as compared to earlier, back in Ryman Springs, when he wasn't such a heavy load?

"No, thank you. I can manage."

"You look flushed. Instead of walking, why don't we just sit on that rock over there in the shade? You can look in your big book and tell me what that cactus with the thorny tentacles is called."

His hand on her elbow nudged Beth toward the rock, and, while at the moment she did prefer shade to the hot walk, she was not about to open the book and reveal that without removing the glasses she could not distinguish a cactus from a caterpillar. Was he testing her again, because he suspected the glasses were as phony as her name?

She shoved the book at him after they sat on the rock. "You look."

"Very well." He removed the sunglasses and tucked them in his shirt pocket. After a few minutes of searching in the book he announced that the plant was an *ocotillo*. "But it isn't really a cactus. When there's enough moisture it puts out tiny green leaves, and it's a shrub."

"Does that fine distinction really matter when you're punctured by one of its thorns?" Beth muttered. She was still annoyed at finding herself alone with him, not inclined toward sweet graciousness in a situation she was certain he had deliberately contrived.

He laughed at her tart remark. "Perhaps not."

He went on leafing through the big book, identifying the huge, blunt-armed cactus as *saguaro*, the tree with smooth, green bark as *palo verde*, another tree as *mesquite*, and the cactus that looked soft and cuddly as golden fuzz…but wasn't!…as *cholla*.

"I love those names," Beth said, her defenses momentarily lowered by the interesting but non-threatening information. "They sound so exotic."

Guy laughed again. "Here's one that isn't so exotic. That big

114

bird we saw earlier, the long-tailed one that could run so fast? He's called a roadrunner."

Beth laughed too. "How appropriate." She removed the glasses and pretended to rub a speck off the lens, but she also snatched a brief, clear glimpse of him. The feather and rakish tilt of the straw hat gave him an appealing, almost boyish innocence...but a small hint of mischievousness as well. A far less somber and hostile aura than he'd had when she encountered him back in Ryman Springs.

But it was an appeal she must be on guard against! She must not forget, no matter how congenial and friendly he pretended to be, that he was a danger to her and Joey. But in spite of that, she found herself unexpectedly curious about him. Where did he live in Phoenix? What did he do outside work on the newspaper? How interested was he in Gillian? But she grabbed another neutral question instead, to avoid a perilous slip into the personal. "Is there really a buried treasure out here?"

"There are various wild tales from back in the eighteen hundreds about an old prospector known as the Lost Dutchman who brought out some gold and claimed he had a fabulous mine somewhere back in these mountains. A number of people have looked for it without success. Although there are plenty of old, abandoned mines hidden all over Arizona. Dangerous places, actually. The skeleton of some unfortunate prospector was found in one only a few weeks ago."

"Gold is a rather...transitory treasure," Beth mused. She shifted to a more comfortable position on the rock, one leg growing numb under Joey's weight.

"Once I'd have argued that point with you," he reflected, "but I've been doing a lot of thinking lately." Unexpectedly he smoothed a rebellious wisp of Joey's hair with his fingertips, hair that was already showing signs of turning from pale baby blond to Guy's own darker bronze-gold. "This is the real treasure."

The statement alarmed Beth, because it sounded so much more personally focused than some general children-are-our-greatest-treasure philosophy. She hastily turned the subject back to the desert plant life. "I wonder what this scrubby green bush is?" She rubbed a leaf of a common, dark-leafed shrub that grew everywhere on the desert. The crushed leaf smelled faintly medicinal and felt oily on her fingertips.

Guy didn't rush to locate it in the book. Instead he said, "You seem as lacking in knowledge about the desert as I am, Mrs. Thompson. Are you also new to the area?"

His tone was casual, but Beth stiffened. She recognized now what he was doing: sneaking up on her with harmless-sounding conversation, luring her into a trap. And then he'd pounce to expose her as a phony, and claim Joey! The perspiration that dampened the thick hair clinging to her temples and ran in unladylike trickles from under her arms had more to do with fear than desert heat.

Yet with rigid back and fierce determination, she forced herself to hide an incriminating panic and say calmly, "Yes, I am relatively new here." She repeated her manufactured story of husband dying of tuberculosis and her move from Seattle to Phoenix.

She ran a trembling finger over Joey's precious little curve of baby ear and whispered an inward prayer, asking for forgiveness—again—for telling the lie. Then she sighed, awaiting Guy's scornful attack. *Oh, come on, that story is as flimsy as cotton candy. We both know you're Bethany Curtis, and this is my nephew Joseph.*

But the dreaded words didn't come. Instead he said politely, "Your baby's name is Joey, didn't you say? Is that short for something?"

"It's just Joey." And how glad she was now that she'd called him Joseph and never used the nickname around Guy back in Ryman Springs!

"How old is he?"

"Not quite a year." She wasn't about to provide the clue of a birth date exactly the same as his nephew's.

"You seem very good with children. You've had a lot of experience, I take it?"

Again she evaded an exact answer. "Some."

"As a governess, or in some other line?" he prodded.

Beth hesitated, growing ever more uneasy with the increasingly pointed interrogation. He could find out from Gillian that she'd claimed prior teaching experience, so deviating from that truth now might only undermine the foundation of her story. "I was a teacher," she said carefully, "but I prefer working as a governess so I can also be a full-time mother to Joey."

"I have a nephew about Joey's age." Guy studied Joey's round little face as if he were pinpointing similarities to that nephew, and the abrupt words whizzed at Beth like both challenge and accusation.

Angrily she turned to face him. It was on the tip of her tongue to issue her own challenge: *If you want to call me a phony, why don't you just do it, instead of playing this coy cat-and-mouse game? Get it over with!* She snatched off the glasses defiantly. But what she saw in Guy's expression wasn't scornful accusation; it was the faint drawing together of bronze-gold eyebrows as if he were trying to solve a complicated puzzle, plus a cloud of uncertainty in his gray eyes.

She plopped the glasses back on her face, momentarily confused. Then the revelation of truth hit her.

Guy was skeptical of her identity as Mrs. Thompson; he strongly suspected she was indeed Bethany Curtis. But he wasn't certain!

A wave of relief mixed with triumph rolled through her. So he was suspicious. Did that really matter? So he was probing and fishing for information. *So what!*

Unless she made the bedrock mistake of admitting her real identity, he had absolutely no way to prove she was Bethany Curtis or that the baby sleeping in her arms was his father's grandson. Even if he openly accused her, all she need do was stand her ground, look puzzled and astonished at such a strange charge, and deny everything. The truth was not, after all, engraved on her forehead! And she didn't need to run again, because Guy wouldn't risk snatching the wrong child. Just think how furious bloodline-minded Nat Wilkerson would be if Guy presented him with a baby but could offer no assurance that it was the right one.

Unexpected giddiness flooded through her after the first wave of relief. She felt like tossing those ridiculous glasses high in the air and doing a little dance of joy beneath them. She needn't skulk around trying to keep out of Guy's sight, needn't fearfully avert her gaze every time he looked at her. It was like discovering a heretofore unknown opening in the prison walls of apprehension that had enclosed her ever since discovering Guy was in Phoenix. And it was time to have a little *fun* on this picnic!

"I'm going back and stick my feet in one of those pools of water," she declared with a newfound, lighthearted gaiety. On impulse she looked Guy square in the eye and added with spirited challenge, "Care to join me?"

Guy followed the auburn-haired governess back to their picnic area, puzzled by the abrupt change in her, the sudden leap from a nervous, scared-rabbit ducking of her head every time he looked at her to lively new exuberance. He retraced the past few minutes in which he had carefully steered their conversation from the subject of desert flora and fauna to casual questions about her, but he now found no more clues to the change in her demeanor than he had found to her identity during the course of the conversation. But something had definitely happened.

Was she Bethany Curtis or Mrs. Annie Thompson? At the moment he was more uncertain than ever.

But as he watched her at the edge of the shallow pool as she gaily tossed her shoes aside and tied the skirt of that shapeless uniform into a knot to keep the hem out of the water, his main thought was that, whoever she was, he liked what he saw. A sweet and lovely young woman, more attractive than ever with this hint of vivacious high spirits about her. She called to the twins, who were mischievously poking at an anthill with silver forks from the picnic basket, to join her. A moment later all three were in the water, the governess wading like a carefree child herself, gaily dipping baby Joey's little feet in the water too. Yes, he decided impulsively, he was indeed going to join them!

"Guy, would you come over here, please?" Gillian called.

For the last few minutes, Guy had actually forgotten Gillian's presence. Now he saw that she was sitting in the car, all four doors open to catch a nonexistent breeze. She looked hot, disgruntled, and hostile enough to poke silver forks at *him*.

Reluctantly he turned away from the laughter and splashing at the shallow pool and approached the car.

"I'm ready to leave now," Gillian stated.

"It's early yet, and the twins are having so much fun—"

"Guy, I want to *go*," Gillian repeated in a tone frigid enough to produce frost on a hot cactus. "*Now,* tell Annie to stop acting so irresponsibly and ridiculously. Have her get the twins out of that filthy water and bring them to the car *immediately.*"

Guy's first reaction when Gillian demanded to leave was guilt. He should have realized, from the way she and the twins were dressed, that she hadn't expected quite this primitive a location for the picnic. And he hadn't been fair with her, he also had to admit, setting up this whole outing, not because he was interested in her, but because he wanted a chance to study and question "Mrs. Thompson." But her royal command that he chastise the governess and relay her stuffy orders definitely ruffled him the wrong way.

"I think I'll just stick my feet in the water and cool off myself," he said, his tone pleasant but unmoved by her demands.

"Guy, I'm warning you—"

He turned. "Yes?"

"Father won't like this," she muttered ungraciously as she gave the car door an angry jab with her high-heeled sandal.

Guy liked working at the newspaper. But he wasn't about to kowtow to Gillian's mean-spirited demands to keep from losing the job. He'd also seen enough of her work as society editor at the newspaper to know that an assistant did most of the real work; Gillian would have been fired months ago if her father were not owner of the newspaper.

He left her fuming like a hot radiator.

At the edge of the shallow pool he took off his shoes and socks and rolled up his pant legs. The twins were now chasing bugs in a lower pool. For all her earlier challenge, Mrs. Thompson…or Bethany?…looked momentarily uneasy when he joined her and the laughing baby in the water. She no doubt expected he would start interrogating her again.

"Feels great, doesn't it?" He wiggled his bare toes appreciatively.

"Yes. Very refreshing. I hadn't expected to find anything like this out here on the desert."

"Let me have Joey's hand."

"Why?"

"We can hold him more steady between us," he pointed out reasonably. "You won't have to worry about slipping on the slick rocks and falling with him."

She apparently saw the wisdom in that, although she seemed reluctant when she transferred the baby's chubby little fist to Guy's hand. They waded around the tiny pool, which reached no higher than his midcalf at the deepest point. Little Joey, bare to his diaper, bounced delightedly in the lukewarm water.

Guy surreptitiously watched the governess out of the corner of his eye. She wasn't wearing the heavy glasses now, although what that meant, if anything, Guy was uncertain. Her short hair was mussed now, quite attractively mussed, actually, and no longer pulled forward around her eyes as if she were trying to hide behind it. And what wonderful blue eyes she had. Bethany-blue eyes, he thought, remembering the first moment he'd seen that same, intense jeweled blue back in Oklahoma.

"Bethany," he said softly.

She was half-turned away from him, her free hand reaching for an interesting pebble on a ledge of rock above the water. He didn't intend the softly breathed word as a trap; it had simply come out naturally, because at that moment he was certain she was Bethany. Yet even as the name passed his lips, he realized that the element of surprise offered a small test.

Did she stiffen at the sound of the name? Clutch little Joey's hand so tightly that he gave a squeal of protest? She instantly knelt, unmindful of the knotted skirt dipping into the water, to nuzzle and comfort him. She looked up at Guy without acknowledging the name he'd just spoken.

"I heard Gillian say she wanted to leave, and perhaps it's time—"

"Bethany, I don't want you to be afraid of me," he said quickly. "I'm not here to harm or endanger you."

If his use of the name startled her, she gave no sign of it. Nor did she give any sign of relief at his assurance of safety. She simply lifted the wet baby into her arms and said with a note of bewilderment, "Pardon?"

"I know who you are, Bethany." But even as he spoke the words, his brief certainty crumbled. No, he did *not* know. She was looking so baffled that he felt almost foolish. Was she a great actress, or had he really made a clumsy mistake?

He'd been so certain he could make a positive identification today, but his scheme to count freckles had failed, foiled by a smooth, honey-rose tan that, if there were any freckles, effectively concealed all traces of them. And stubborn evasion on her part had effectively thwarted his attempts to dig information out of her.

If she *wasn't* Bethany, it wasn't surprising that she'd think him very odd, calling her a strange name and mumbling assurances about not being afraid of him. If she *was* Bethany, she had to be terrified that he'd identified her. In either case, it was no surprise that she was now sheltering the baby against her chest, slim arms wrapped tightly around him and eyes blazing with a fierce protectiveness.

"Guy, I would like to leave now," Gillian interrupted in a petulant call from the car.

"Okay. In a minute," he called back. He hesitated, uncertain whether to demand an admission of truth from the woman facing him so defiantly or to apologize for his error. Finally, all he did was mutter, "I'll get the twins."

He rounded them up and returned them to the picnic blanket, where the governess cleaned them with a wet napkin and dried them with a corner of the blanket. She retrieved the silver forks from the anthill, and he loaded the wicker basket into the trunk strapped to the luggage rack of the Packard. Gillian just sat in the car with her arms folded. Eye makeup, melting in the heat, smudged her cheek. When the twins ran over to climb in the backseat of the car they were reasonably clean and dry, but Ariana's once-crisp dress now hung limply, and Adrian had a rip in his pants. They were also wildly happy about their day's adventures, enthusiastically telling their mother about bugs and lizards, and begging for another picnic.

"We'll see," Gillian said. To the governess, who had put the baby in the car and was now shaking and folding the blankets, she called, "Annie, come here. I want to talk to you."

The governess, who had been laughing with the twins a moment earlier, stopped smiling as she approached the car. Guy could see why. Gillian's look was hostile enough to intimidate a guard dog.

"Annie, how you have let the children behave today is absolutely outrageous." Gillian's tone was low and furious. "They're filthy and disheveled and their clothes ruined, and I will not stand for the irresponsible attitude you have displayed today. When we get back to the house, you will pack your things and get out immediately."

"I'm fired?" the governess asked, her dismay obvious. "But you can't expect children on a picnic to sit around like porcelain dolls."

"I've also had quite enough of your insubordination," Gillian snapped.

Guy stepped up to the open door. "Hey, wait a minute," he protested. He hadn't seen any "insubordination," and the governess was right: two energetic kids surely couldn't spend a picnic sitting stiffly on a blanket, primly worrying about keeping their clothes clean. "This isn't fair—"

He broke off, momentarily confused as Gillian's furious gaze swung to target him. What had *he* done?

Oh, but he knew what he'd done, of course. He'd paid far more attention to the children's governess than he had to Gillian herself. And Gillian, though she might be angry at him, was unfairly putting the largest portion of the blame on the governess. That was the real reason for the firing.

He glanced at the governess again. Frankly, he couldn't see why anyone would want to work for someone as petulant, vindictive, and ill-tempered as Gillian. But from the governess's taut expression and death grip on the car door, she apparently wanted this position desperately.

Guy made himself chuckle as if this were some just-in-fun joke. "My dear Gillian," he said as he reached through the open door and rubbed the back of her neck lightly. "What a lovely little spitfire you are when you're angry. Such beautiful, flashing eyes! I think what you and I need is a glass of good wine, a fine dinner at some downtown restaurant, and a relaxing evening at a movie. All far removed from hot sun and rocks and cactuses."

Gillian hesitated but then melted under the compliments and invitation, her vanity apparently willing to accept that his romantic interest was really in her after all. "That does sound lovely."

"And there's really no reason to let Mrs. Thompson go," he added persuasively. "I'm sure a single day's lapse in her excellent care of the children can be forgiven."

Gillian nodded, dismissing her earlier harsh words with a small, regal wave of a manicured hand, although she dropped a final warning. "We'll let it go, then. For now."

The governess went around the rear of the car to reach the

back door on the far side. He circled the hood to reach the driver's door. They met at the open doors.

"Thank you," she said in a voice low enough to escape Gillian's hearing. "I appreciate your putting in a word to save my job for me."

He was doing more than that, Guy thought wryly to himself. He had committed himself to having dinner and spending an entire evening with Gillian to save the job. But all he did was murmur, "You're welcome."

"It's been a lovely picnic," she added a bit awkwardly. "Thank you for that, too."

"I meant to talk to you about Seattle but never got around to it. It's such a beautiful area, all those forests and mountains. I spent some time there on business a couple of years ago."

"Yes, it is lovely."

"I especially liked watching the rose and gold sunsets on Mount Hood."

"Yes, I always enjoyed that too."

"And watching a storm roll in across Tacoma Sound."

She hesitated a moment and then nodded agreement. "Quite spectacular."

She slid inside the car, and he closed the door for her. It wasn't fair, he thought guiltily, tricking her when she was upset and distracted about almost losing her job, and also feeling grateful to him for saving it. But his carefully worded remarks had served their purpose.

You're smart and clever, he thought as he angled the rearview mirror to get a glimpse of her in the backseat. *Courageous, too. But you should have boned up on your Seattle-area geography.* One error might not have proven anything. But two?

Her wary eyes briefly met his in the mirror. He smiled.

Hello, Miss Bethany Curtis.

Eleven

Guy yanked off his tie as he opened the door to the cramped apartment he'd rented a few days after arriving in Phoenix. The lace curtains hung limp and motionless in spite of the open windows, and the warm air smelled of the onions the couple in the next apartment were always cooking. But he was grateful for the quiet spot in which to retreat alone.

Bethany Curtis, he said to himself, *I hope you appreciate the sacrifice I made for you tonight!*

Not that many men wouldn't be delighted to squire Gillian around, he supposed. She was beautiful enough to draw second glances wherever they went. She knew her way around fashionable clothes, fine wine, and good food. She could be witty and amusing.

She was also relentlessly self-centered, an acid-tongued gossip, possessively clingy, and a more ambitious social-climber than his sister-in-law back in St. Louis. And if his head wasn't already throbbing with the strain of being charming and attentive, he'd do a little dance of joy that the evening with her was over.

He was also grateful that he would not have to repeat the experience. He smiled as he draped his silk tie over a chair. He'd confided a few facts about himself to Gillian following the movie, after which, when he suggested lunch the next week, she'd suddenly remembered a calendar overflowing with previous engagements. He should have been insulted at the speed with which she'd dropped him from her list of eligible suitors, he thought with wry amusement, but he was too relieved that she'd reacted exactly as he'd expected when he made his little revelation.

The important question now that he'd helped Gillian dump him was, how was he going to see Bethany again?

He considered that problem as he showered. He couldn't follow the usual course of a man interested in an attractive woman and simply call her up and invite her out for dinner or a movie. She'd simply decline. There was no chance of encountering her at some social event…especially now that he was definitely off Gillian's list of desirable guests.

A problem. But not one he intended to give up on.

He started to switch off the lamp after he threw back the covers on the bed, but on second thought picked up the Bible on the nightstand. He scrunched the pillow into a lumpy ball and leaned back against the wooden headboard.

Long ago he could recite all the books of both the Old and New Testaments, but now his mind went blank after Deuteronomy, and he had to use the index to locate Proverbs. He read through the chapters that Bethany…he could confidently call her that in his mind now…had suggested, and there it was, the verse he had fruitlessly searched for, Proverbs 22:6. "Train up a child in the way he should go: and when he is old, he will not depart from it."

He stuck a finger in the pages to keep his place as he reflected on the words and gazed out the open window at the sliver of crescent moon rising in the east. Training up Joey in the way he should go was what Bethany intended, of course. Would she be successful? He thought about himself, his own childhood. He had, though it had not been a lengthy experience, been "trained up" by Mrs. Sommersby in Christian belief. Would that early training influence him now that he was "old"? A few months ago he'd have laughed at the idea that he still held any of those beliefs, but now, out from under the powerful influence of Nat's scorn of anything "religious," things were looking different.

He leafed idly through the gilt-edged pages, occasionally encountering a verse or two familiar from long ago, more often finding himself curious and intrigued by something he'd never seen before.

It was almost midnight before he set the Bible aside and turned off the lamp. He was on the edge of sleep before he realized he'd gotten sidetracked from the question he'd asked himself earlier.

How would he manage to see Bethany again? He had to make it happen, of course; hoping for some accidental encounter wouldn't do it.

And there was one place he could encounter her, one place from which she surely wouldn't try to run him off, even if she was so inclined.

A week had passed since the desert picnic. Beth sat in the pew of the small church listening to the organ prelude of "In the Garden," Joey bouncing on her lap and playing a gurgly peek-aboo with a woman in the pew behind them. The twins weren't with her today; Mr. Gardiner had taken them on a weekend trip with him to visit a ranch he owned, with a promise they could ride a horse.

Pastor Merriman had just stepped up to the pulpit to offer an opening prayer when a dark-suited man, ignoring the almost empty pew two rows ahead, squeezed into the narrow space between Beth and the end of her pew. She had only a brief moment to glance at him before closing her eyes for the prayer, but it was enough to jolt her with a startled identification.

Guy Wilkerson!

What was he doing here? What devious scheme was he concocting now? How had he located the church she attended?

She wanted to demand answers, but she couldn't during the service, of course. He made no effort to speak to her, merely offering a smile when their hands collided as they reached for the same hymnal.

She kept her attention on the message, but never for a moment was she not aware of his presence. The faint scent of some expensive aftershave lotion. The deep strength of his voice singing "Amazing Grace" as if he were quite familiar with it. The smooth feel of his suit and the solid breadth of the muscle beneath when his shoulder brushed hers. It did not help that baby Joey was uncharacteristically interested in transferring himself from her lap to Guy's, and she kept having to pull him back.

She couldn't help but notice the discreetly folded bill Guy put in the collection plate amidst the modest coins given by the working-class members of this church. At the same time, she thought briefly of the abrupt and puzzling change in Gillian's attitude toward him. Where only a couple of weeks earlier Gillian had appeared quite smitten with him, now she disdainfully brushed him off as a "common nobody." He wasn't even on the guest list of the next dinner party Gillian was planning, a rather hurried affair she'd put together for this coming Tuesday evening.

After the service he still didn't say anything as they made their way slowly toward the door, Guy the recipient of many curious glances that he blandly ignored. When they reached Pastor Merriman standing at the door, courtesy forced Beth to make an introduction.

"Mr. Wilkerson." Pastor Merriman heartily repeated the name as he shook hands with Guy. She hadn't offered his first name. "We're happy to have you with us today and hope you'll come again."

"Thank you. I may do that."

Outside, where the first-week-of-June heat was rising, Beth gave no further acknowledgment of Guy's presence. She had decided not to demand answers; she would simply ignore him. She put Joey in the baby buggy which she had left, as usual, just around the corner from the main entrance.

"I can give you a ride home," Guy offered.

"I have the baby buggy."

"I can strap it on the luggage rack."

"No, thank you." She gave the buggy a brisk push toward the sidewalk. "I enjoy the walk."

"Very well, I'll walk with you."

That stopped her. "That doesn't make sense. You'll just have to walk back here to get your car. And it's getting hot."

"I don't mind." He took off his jacket and loosened his tie as if he were prepared for a long hike.

She started walking. He strode along beside her. Baby Joey made the only attempt at communication, a repeating grunt that meant he'd like to go faster. Beth maintained a sedate pace.

Finally Guy said, "The pastor gave a fine message today."

Pastor Merriman tended to stick to the basics, and today's message had been from that most basic and essential of Bible verses, John 3:16. And, yes, it had been a fine message. "Did you come to hear the message?" she challenged.

"No," he admitted. "I came because I wanted to talk to you and didn't know any other way to do it. I figured you were too good a Christian to be rude to me in church." He paused and added reflectively, "Although I've been thinking I might start attending church somewhere anyway."

"We aren't in church now," she pointed out.

"Are you going to be rude to me?"

"I'm not certain it would do any good," she grumbled. "How did you find out which one was my church?"

"I parked down the street from the house, waited until you came out, and followed you at a distance. Although I almost lost you a time or two when you cut down an alley or behind a building." He grinned. "You pilot that baby buggy like I used to maneuver a race car."

The teasing compliment embarrassed her, but more important was the fact that she had thought she was still being reasonably careful about possible Wilkerson spies, yet she hadn't even noticed him following her!

"No wonder you managed to lose me in Ft. Worth," he added. "Although it is too bad you had to cut off your beautiful long hair to disguise yourself, Bethany."

With determined self-control she forced herself to shake her head as if bewildered. "Why do you keep calling me that name? Why are you saying all these strange things about Ft. Worth and my hair?"

He laughed cheerfully. "We both know why."

Yes. She'd made a disastrous slip at the desert picnic. She'd managed to halt a giveaway reaction when he tried to trick her by unexpectedly calling her by her real name, but he'd trapped her with his sleight-of-tongue remarks about the Seattle area. She honestly hadn't recognized the wrong mountain he'd named. Tacoma Sound hadn't sounded quite right, but she wasn't positive enough to say anything at the time. But after she'd gotten home she'd looked into a reference book in Mr. Gardiner's library and immediately found how Guy had slyly tricked her. Mt. Rainier, not Mt. Hood, could be seen from Seattle; Mt. Hood was miles away in Oregon. And Tacoma was the name of a nearby city, not the body of salt water flanking Seattle. That was Puget Sound.

So what? she now asked herself defiantly. Yes, she should have protected her Seattle-widow story by familiarizing herself with facts about the area, but she still was not about to admit she was Bethany Curtis, no matter how many sneaky tricks Guy pulled!

"I'm afraid I don't know what you're talking about, Mr. Wilkerson," she said politely.

"Guy," he suggested. "By the way, has Gillian mentioned me since last week?"

"A time or two."

He laughed again. "Not fondly or flatteringly, I'll wager. After the movie on Saturday, I confessed to her that I am no longer one of the rich and powerful Wilkersons of St. Louis. My father and I had a rather hostile falling-out, and I fear I am, alas, no longer in line to inherit a share of the family wealth."

Beth's surprised gaze jumped to his. Was that true?

"I am now, I admitted to her, just plain Guy Wilkerson, cub reporter. I had the impression that Gillian was…ah…somewhat disappointed to hear this. She was suddenly much too busy to see me again." He pulled an excessively mournful face. "I'm heartbroken, of course."

It was all Beth could do not to burst out laughing. He was so obviously *not* heartbroken, and was, in fact, himself laughing at Gillian's transparent change in attitude toward him. So he

132

hadn't been taken in by her shallow sweetness after all! But she managed to keep her laughter to herself and say gravely, "You have my most sincere sympathies."

"Thank you." He was equally grave, but his mouth twitched with good humor.

She hesitated and then asked cautiously, "Was what you told Gillian true?"

"Yes. Quite true. I've separated myself completely from both the family and the Wilkerson business enterprises."

"Why?"

"A matter of some differences with my father that could not be compromised. I've long wanted to get into newspaper work, and this seemed an appropriate time to do it."

"I'm surprised, in these hard times, that without experience you could find a newspaper job."

"The fact that I volunteered to work without pay while learning the ropes may have had something to do with it."

So he wasn't exactly penniless, Beth realized, her interior warning signals buzzing again. This could be just another trick to deceive her into trusting him. And if, in spite of her denials, he was now positive she was Bethany Curtis, and the baby his nephew, Joseph, would he be bold enough to snatch Joey after all?

As if reading her thoughts he unexpectedly put an arm around her shoulders. For a moment the solid grip felt temptingly protective, but she instantly discarded that dangerous idea and twisted away from him.

"Look, I'm not going to demand that you admit to me that you're Bethany Curtis. You want to keep on claiming to be Annie Thompson, widow from Seattle, fine. But I have a few things to say, and I intend that you listen even if I have to put both arms around you right here on the street and hold you still until you do listen."

"That won't be necessary," Beth said with alarm, thinking he was capable of doing exactly what he said.

"Okay, what I have to say is this. After I lost your trail in Ft. Worth, my father hired a detective agency to find you. It took them awhile, what with the detour of a wild-goose chase in the Chicago area—" He paused and smiled at what he apparently considered a clever ploy on her part. "But they finally uncovered your disguise and traced you here to Phoenix. The last communication I saw from the detective said they were very close to pinpointing your exact location."

The man who had made inquiries to Mrs. Welsch…and had sent Beth herself on that wild, cross-town flight one night!

"But before I left St. Louis, I canceled the investigation. By then I was convinced Sylvia's baby belonged with you, not my father. I told the agency we were no longer interested in you and to end the search immediately. I then altered the communication from the agency to inform my father that you had left the country and further search for you would be futile."

Beth took an astonished moment to absorb his bold maneuverings on her behalf. Then she asked pointedly, "And so why, Mr. Wilkerson, are *you* here?"

"I was getting out of St. Louis. Phoenix looked as good as anywhere." He paused. "Actually, that isn't the whole truth, of course. I'm here because of you and Joey. Because I wanted to let you know you were no longer in danger and do whatever I could to help you." He hesitated again and then added with a soft bluntness that made her breath catch, "And also because I find you very attractive and wanted to see you again."

"That's very interesting, Mr. Wilkerson." She did not call him Guy, and, after a swallow, added carefully, "If I were this Bethany you think I am, I'd be most flattered."

134

"I understand your reluctance to admit to being Bethany. I can understand that you might not want to place your full trust in me yet. But if you'll give me a chance I'll prove that you *can* trust me."

At which point, Beth thought warily, what might be proved was the opposite, that she *couldn't* trust him. But by then it would be too late.

And even if everything he said were true, she reflected uneasily, she and Joey were not out of danger.

"Let's say, just for the matter of discussion, that you can be trusted," Beth suggested slowly, feeling her way through her own maze of apprehension. "You've had a change of heart, broken with your father, and called off the investigation of this Bethany Curtis, so you can now assure her she's safe, that you aren't going to take her baby away from her."

He grabbed her shoulders and whirled her around to face him. "Bethany, I *know* who you are. Keep up the pretense with everyone else if you want, but please, not with me. I want to help, not hurt you."

Did he? Yes, she could almost believe, staring into the fierce silver intensity of his eyes, that Guy didn't intend to snatch Joey or betray her to his father. Which was still a long way from meaning she and Joey were safe.

"But has your father also had a change of heart?"

"No, but he's too swamped with serious business problems to think of much of anything else."

"But at some point your father and this detective agency *are* going to get together again. They're going to compare notes and figure out what you did. And then what?"

Twelve

❦

The entire building vibrated when the daily run of the printing presses began. Most people outside the newspaper business hated the noisy clatter and rumble. Even some within the business were not fond of it. But it exhilarated Guy, just as almost everything about putting out a newspaper exhilarated him, from digging up the news to sitting at his cramped desk pounding out the words on a typewriter. He liked watching the Linotype operator cope with the temperamental complexities of the typesetting equipment, liked hearing the impudent chatter of a newsboy hawking copies, and he'd never forget the thrill of spying a man at a coffee shop actually reading something he'd written.

He liked to run down and grab one of the first copies as it rolled off the press, the sharp smell of ink still fresh on the page, even though he had to search back on pages four or five to find his own stories. He covered the routine court and police reports, but the top reporter, "Scotch" Wiseman, got any crime stories important enough to warrant a position on the front page.

But today would be different! The piece he'd written after dashing back from the police station this morning might not garner a banner headline, but it should make page one. It was *news*.

After pausing to savor the moment of excitement when the presses started up, Guy began typing again, working on a human interest piece about an old Navajo woman weaver he'd met while wandering a shabby area of town. He paused again when Ben from the wire services room tossed him a torn scrap of paper.

"This just came in. Thought you might be interested."

Guy could guess the subject matter even before he saw the St. Louis dateline. Before Gillian dropped him, she'd apparently spread the word that he was connected to the rich and powerful Wilkersons of St. Louis. Now Ben, a nice guy who no doubt thought he was being helpful, always routed Guy a copy of any Wilkerson-connected news.

Actually, those occasional bits of news had been helpful. He'd meant it when he warned his father he wasn't going to let him get away with arson or violence, and through the wire service releases he'd been able to keep an eye on the Wilkerson activities.

Now Guy's gaze flicked across the few lines of print. "Without preliminary announcement, the Wilkerson Textile Mills abruptly closed its doors today, putting an estimated four hundred people out of work." The release went on to say that owner Nat Wilkerson was not available for comment, and there was no word on whether the closure was expected to be temporary or permanent.

Guy sympathized with all the mill workers hurt by loss of their jobs, but the sympathy did not extend to his father. Nat had long scrimped on everything from wages to safety measures at the mill, his concern only for profits. And Nat was surely now too swamped with business problems to give much thought to Bethany and his grandson.

But the time was coming when Nat would target them again; Bethany had been right about that. Guy could only wonder now why he had blithely assumed what he'd done would assure her safety indefinitely. Sooner or later, Nat would resume the hunt.

He had a sudden, overwhelming need to talk to her, to assure himself that she was still safe. He didn't yet rate a telephone on his desk, and rather than use someone else's he ran out to the street to call from the pay phone a half block away. The relief he felt when she answered the ring with a cultured, "Gardiner residence," was also overwhelming.

Carefully he did not use her real name. "Annie, this is Guy Wilkerson."

A moment of silence before she said warily, "I'm sorry but neither Mr. Gardiner nor Gillian are home just now."

"I wasn't calling either of them. I was calling you." He felt rather foolish now, hearing her calm and secure. Lamely he added, "I had a sudden feeling of…concern about you."

"I'm fine." But the most infinitesimal of hesitations alerted him that perhaps all was not fine after all.

"Are you sure?"

Another tiny hesitation before she said, "It's nothing, really. Just that this morning I had set up my easel in the backyard and was painting while the children played, and a…I guess you'd call him a hobo…came looking for a handout."

The nervousness in Bethany's voice concerned him more than her actual words. Desperate, out-of-work men were everywhere these days, more to be sympathized with than feared. He slipped coins or a folded bill to one every once in a while. But suddenly he also felt a surprise rush of encouragement. She had trusted him enough to reveal this worry; she hadn't openly admitted her identity, but unspoken between them was the understanding that she was afraid this hobo might have some connection with the detective agency and Nat Wilkerson.

"I doubt there's anything to be worried about," he assured her. "He was probably just someone passing through, down on his luck."

"That's what I keep telling myself. But we're a long way from the railroad and main highway, and even after I made a sandwich for him, he kept hanging around, looking at my painting. And darting little glances at Joey."

Would Blacketer send an investigator disguised as a hobo? *Why not?* Perhaps Nat wasn't too tied up with business problems to ignore Bethany and his grandson after all.

"I'd really like to see you again," he said urgently. "I think we should talk about this."

She hesitated, and he thought she was going to decline. But instead, even though there was a note of wariness in her voice, she finally said, "I have Wednesday evenings off. I usually go to midweek services at church, but they've been discontinued for the summer."

"Seven o'clock Wednesday evening, then. I'll take you and Joey to dinner. No, make that six o'clock." He wanted to spend every minute he could with her.

"That will be fine. Thank you."

Thank *you*, Lord.

Guy stopped short as he replaced the receiver. *Thank you, Lord?* Since when had he started thanking the Lord for anything?

Since he'd vaguely started realizing that the Lord was moving in his life, that actions and circumstances he might once have attributed to accident or fate were actually under God's control.

Yes, thank you, Lord! This time he added a special plea, the first true prayer he'd offered in a long time. *And show me what to do to protect Bethany and Joey. Help me to figure out how to keep them safe.*

He went back to his desk, finished his article on the Indian weaver, and dropped it in the managing editor's box before dashing down to the printing press to pick up a copy of today's paper. He stood in the hallway skimming the headlines, disappointed that his important piece wasn't on the front page, surprised when it wasn't on page two, and angry when he realized it hadn't been printed at all.

He started to toss the paper away, then changed his mind and charged back up to the managing editor's office. He stormed in without knocking. "What happened to my piece on Cavanaugh?" he demanded.

Walt Wyman, big, bald, and brawny, looking more like the corner butcher than a newspaperman, glanced up from the typewritten pages Guy had written minutes earlier. "We didn't run it."

"I can see that!" Guy slapped the folded newspaper on the desk. "What I don't understand is *why.* The man is on the city council. He was involved in a hit and run accident and arrested driving drunk, and he was in the company of a woman of questionable morals. If that isn't *news,* I don't know what is!"

"I didn't feel it would be in the best interest to print it." Walt calmly flipped a typewritten page and continued reading.

"*Whose* best interest? His? Yours? Certainly not the public's! The voters and taxpayers have a right to know what kind of man has a hand on the reins of city management."

"I decided not to print it, and my decision is final."

"Does Gardiner know about your decisions on these matters? That you censor unfavorable news about your big shot friends, or anyone you figure can do you a favor if you keep his ugly back-street doings out of the newspaper?"

The accusations were a shot in the dark, but Guy knew he'd hit a bull's-eye when Walt's pale, bald head suddenly turned florid. Walt deflected the accusations with an odd accusation of his own.

"Gardiner doesn't know any more about running a newspaper than I know about flying to the moon. You know how he got to be owner? He loaned the former owner money, and when the man couldn't pay, Gardiner wound up with the newspaper. The only reason he kept it was because his darling daughter decided she wanted to play society editor."

Guy doubted he rated any higher in Walt's esteem than Gillian did. Rumor had it that Walt had played the stock market and lost almost everything in the '29 crash, and bitterly resented anyone who still had money. Where once Walt had appreciated Guy's willingness to work without pay to learn the newspaper business, now he scorned him as a rich kid playing reporter.

Guy nodded toward the pages spread out on Walt's desk. "What about my piece on the Navajo woman?"

Walt shrugged. "Who wants to read about some old woman sitting in her dirt yard weaving Indian blankets?"

"That old woman is sitting there, practically destitute, because we, our government, have stolen from her and her people, mistreated them, shoved them around, lied to them."

"I print news that sells newspapers," Walt growled. "Take your soapbox somewhere else."

"This is no way to run a newspaper! A newspaper has influence, and along with influence comes responsibility."

Walt smiled maliciously, deliberately squashed the typewritten pages into a crumpled ball, and tossed it in Guy's direction. Guy let it fall to the floor and stalked out.

Gardiner was a decent man in most ways. He treated Bethany and Joey fairly. He apparently knew nothing of his managing editor's censorship of certain news items. He might be forgiven for indulging his daughter's whim. But he was no newspaperman, and this was no way to run a newspaper.

And while he was on that subject, why weren't Gardiner and Walt purchasing modern photoengraving equipment so they could print photos immediately instead of having to send them out for the time-consuming process of making zinc cuts?

If this were *his* newspaper...

Thirteen

❧

"Oh, Mrs. Thompson, I must speak with you!"

Beth turned at the sound of the breathless voice. Ariana and Adrian had just sung a little song for the dinner party guests, and Beth was herding the pair toward the stairs. "Yes?"

The stout woman in expensive aqua silk rushed up like a friendly barge churning upstream. Gillian disparagingly called the prominent society woman a "fat cow" in private, but Mrs. Dubuque also had an eligible son out in San Francisco who interested Gillian.

"I was just asking Harold who did that lovely painting of the twins, and he said it was *you.*"

The painting, which Mr. Gardiner had taken to an art shop for framing in elaborate gilt, now hung prominently over the fireplace in the living room.

"Such a talent you have, my dear!" Mrs. Dubuque gushed. "You've captured the children's innocence and mischievousness perfectly. And such marvelous, natural skin tones!"

"Thank you. Children are my favorite subjects."

Out of the corner of her eye Beth saw that Gillian was eavesdropping on this conversation, and she knew it presented

Gillian with a problem. Gillian didn't like seeing her governess garner such lavish praise, but if credit was to be given for discovery of talent, she didn't want to lose out on claiming it. Gillian solved the dilemma by rushing over and taking credit for the children themselves.

"Sometimes I still can't believe such beautiful, adorable children are really mine." Gillian ruffled the twin heads with a fine show of motherly affection, never noticing Ariana's indignation at having her hair mussed in public.

"I was wondering, Mrs. Thompson, if you are available for other portraits? I'd love to have a painting done of my granddaughter."

Here it was, a step toward fulfilling her dream that someday she'd be able to make a living with her painting! "Oh, I'd be—"

"That's very flattering of you, Martha," Gillian cut in, "but I'm afraid our Annie is much too busy with the twins to take on any outside projects." Gillian squeezed an arm around Beth's waist as if she were some cherished and indispensable member of the family.

Disappointed, Beth didn't know what to say. She hated to lose this opportunity, but Gillian was right. So long as she was a full-time governess, her primary responsibility was to the twins.

"Oh, come now, Gillian…" Mr. Gardiner unexpectedly strode toward them. "Surely we can give Annie time to accommodate Martha's wishes. Her granddaughter could just come over and play with the twins a time or two, and Annie could paint her then. Would that work, Annie?"

"Yes, I could manage with that." Classic portrait painters might need hours of motionless posing, but Beth, working with baby Joey, other children back in Ryman Springs, and the energetic twins, had developed a more on-the-fly technique.

"Can't see all this talent we have here going to waste," Mr.

Gardiner added magnanimously.

Mrs. Dubuque gushed her thanks, and Beth also thanked him. Gillian frowned her displeasure but remained silent. Beth suspected that Mr. Gardiner's helpful decision wasn't entirely altruistic. He likely planned to use this in furthering some business dealings with Mr. Dubuque. But Beth appreciated the help anyway. She had a commission to do a painting! She could hardly wait to tell Guy.

The unexpected thought astonished her as much as the opportunity to do the painting. Why in the world would she want to tell *him?*

"I'll telephone you later, then, about a convenient time for my granddaughter to come over," Mrs. Dubuque said.

"Annie will be looking forward to hearing from you." Gillian's syrupy tones gave no hint of her annoyance. But the following evening she extracted a small vengeance for what she no doubt considered Beth's new "insubordination."

Beth answered the doorbell herself when Guy arrived. If he felt awkward calling for her here after his brief relationship with Gillian, he didn't show it. He grinned, his gaze approvingly skimming Beth's summery yellow dress before he presented Joey with a combination rattle and teething ring. Joey's blue eyes lit up and he latched onto the gift, enthusiastically babbling his approval.

"I've been looking forward to this all week," Guy said huskily.

"The week is only half over," Beth pointed out.

She had kept reminding herself that this was not really a date, but the warmth in his eyes said it was more than a mere appointment for a discussion.

"It's seemed much longer than half a week, waiting for

tonight." The meaningful tone of his voice sent a message even stronger than the words, a message that both flattered and flustered Beth.

Only then, apparently, did he notice the twins, who were in one of their clingy moods, hanging onto the back of her dress.

"Ariana and Adrian will be coming with us tonight," Beth said quickly. She didn't want to say anything to make the twins feel unwelcome. They got enough of that from Gillian, who was always shooing them off or telling them to wash their hands before they could hug her. "I tried to call you at the newspaper but you'd already gone, and I didn't know where else to reach you."

She could almost have hugged him then, when, instead of grumbling or demanding explanations or postponing dinner he simply said cheerfully, "Well, there isn't going to be any water to splash in or lizards to chase tonight, kids, but I think we can still have fun. What would you two like to eat?"

"Chili!" they chorused unexpectedly, a taste preference taught them by Mr. Gardiner, Beth suspected, because Gillian certainly would not have done so.

Beth suspected Guy had planned something a bit more elegant, but chili it was, in an old railroad caboose transformed into a diner. The chili was delicious, as were the warm tortillas, a food Beth was just learning to appreciate. The twins' spirited chatter and Joey's squirmy wiggles, however, left no opportunity for private conversation between Beth and Guy.

Although once, when the twins were engaged in a giggly and gross discussion about which cow parts the meat in their chili might have come from, Guy leaned across the table of their booth and whispered with a grin, "How many of your own do you want?"

There seemed no proper response to such a teasing, intimate question, so Beth simply made herself very busy helping Joey with a bit of warm tortilla.

When they were all back in the car, Beth thanked Guy for choosing a place to eat that they'd all enjoyed.

He cocked a bronze eyebrow. "You think this is the end of the evening?"

"I presumed—"

"Oh, no. We're just getting started."

He drove a half-mile or so to a schoolhouse, closed now for the summer but with swings and a battered teeter-totter standing idle on the dusty playground. The twins immediately jumped out and claimed the teeter-totter. Beth sat in a swing with Joey in her lap, and Guy gently pushed them back and forth.

Beth felt dreamy and peaceful. The heat of the day still lingered, but trees along the street looped long shadows across the playground. There was an oddly *family* feeling to this outing, very pleasant. She was undecided now whether to tell Guy about the painting for Mrs. Dubuque. She still felt bubbles of excitement, but there was no reason Guy would be interested. "Thanks for being so nice about the twins coming along," she said instead.

"Isn't this supposed to be your evening off?" Guy's question didn't sound like a complaint, merely curiosity.

"Gillian developed a 'blinding headache,' and said she couldn't possibly look after them this evening, that I'd have to do it."

Guy caught the swing and held it back for a moment, his cheek only inches from hers. "And when did she develop this blinding headache?"

"Right after I told her I had an...appointment this evening."

"With me?"

"She asked, so, yes, I told her it was with you."

He laughed and gave the swing a gentle push. "I can see Gillian's scheming little mind working. She was thinking, 'I'll let the twins fix *their* romantic evening.'"

The idea that there was any intent on either her or Guy's part to make this a "romantic evening" was enough to make Beth's cheeks burn. She jumped out of the swing and set Joey on his feet on a patch of scrubby grass.

"We probably should be going home now," she said to cover her embarrassment. Joey had his fist wrapped around her forefinger as he watched the twins banging the teeter-totter and squealing and shrieking. Suddenly he let go, and then, just as if he'd been doing it all his life…

"Guy, look, he's walking!"

"He's not just walking, he's taking a hike!"

It was true. Until now Joey had never done more than toddle a few steps while holding on to someone, but in his eagerness to join the twins he managed a good dozen steps alone before tumbling to the ground and letting out a howl of frustration. Beth ran to him, but Guy swooped him up before she got there.

"Hey, this is no time to cry." He jiggled Joey soothingly. "This is celebration time. You just took your first solo steps!"

Guy's eyes met Beth's over the baby's head as they shared this special moment together. She blinked and brushed a tear from the corner of her eye with her knuckle. It was a wonderful moment, thrilling and happy, and she was pleased Guy was here to share it…and yet sad because Mark and Sylvia weren't.

He surprised her by echoing that thought. "It doesn't seem fair that Sylvia and Mark missed this."

Beth could only swallow and nod. At this moment she felt closer to Guy than she had felt to anyone except baby Joey in a long time. He'd loved his sister just as she'd loved her brother. And they both loved Joey.

"I think he's all worn out now," Guy said. He eased the baby into her arms. "I'll get a blanket from the car."

He spread the blanket on the coarse grass. By this time the twins had abandoned the teeter-totter and were on the swings, their energy still in high gear. Joey scooted into his favorite frog-like sleeping position and immediately fell asleep. Suddenly, feeling so close to Guy, Beth did want to share her other wonderful news. At the last moment she tried to be off-hand as she told about the commission to paint Mrs. Dubuque's granddaughter, as if it wasn't anything terribly important, but Guy wasn't fooled. He reached across the sleeping baby and squeezed her hand in congratulations.

"That's wonderful! With the influential Dubuques showing off your work, you'll be inundated by people wanting to commission you."

Beth laughed self-consciously. She'd had dreamy visions of exactly that herself. Letters and telephone calls from people wanting paintings done by her! Art galleries demanding her work. Lines of people exclaiming over it. But a basically practical nature made her say, "It is a wonderful opportunity, and I'm very grateful for it. But I keep reminding myself, one portrait commission does not make a career. I've never had any real art training. And in these hard times, buying or commissioning a painting is not high on most peoples' list of priorities."

"Don't sell yourself short," he warned. "And don't be afraid to charge Mrs. Dubuque what such a painting is worth. Because you're good, Bethany, you really are. I've always regretted, when I finally realized you'd run out on me in Ryman Springs, that I didn't grab that unfinished painting of Joey you'd left behind."

A taut moment of silence fell between them. Then Beth said

softly, "I was never Bethany to my family or friends. Just Beth."

He sat up slowly, eyes never leaving hers. They both knew what this meant. It was a symbol of her trust, that she was no longer even going through the motions of pretending to be Annie Thompson with him.

"Thank you, Beth." His voice was soft and husky with emotion. "And I want you to know I'll never betray your trust. I'll do everything I can…" He paused and then phrased the promise more emphatically. "I'll do whatever it takes to protect you and Joey from my father."

"Do you think I was being paranoid, fearing that the man who came to the house was something other than a hobo?"

"No, I don't think so." Guy crossed his arms on his knees and looked down at the sleeping baby. "I wouldn't put much of anything past Nat and his sleazy detective."

Beth smiled lightly. "That's exactly what I used to think about you. That I wouldn't put anything past you."

"I'm happy to hear a past tense in that." He scooted a few inches closer on the blanket. "Look, I have an idea. There's a house a few doors down from the Gardiner place with a 'for rent' sign in the window. I'll move out of my apartment and into that house. That way I can keep an eye on you and Joey, and I'll be close if anything happens and you need me."

In spite of the closeness she was feeling toward Guy…or maybe because of it!…the idea of having him living only a few doors away vaguely alarmed Beth. She cast around for an argument against this plan. "I'm afraid renting a house would be much more expensive than an apartment."

"Beth, what I told Gillian about being disinherited by my father was true, and I'm certainly not as well-off financially as I once was. But I'm not exactly headed for the poorhouse. I have various investments and property and assets of my own."

"I see." She hesitated and then said, "But I really don't think it's necessary for you to appoint yourself my watchdog."

He smiled. "I wasn't asking your permission, Beth." He spoke lightly, but with the decisiveness of a falling hammer. He reached across the baby and touched her cheek gently. "I *am* going to rent that house. And I *am* going to be your watchdog."

Guy acted swiftly. Within three days he was living in the house down the street from the Gardiners. It already had a telephone, and he told Beth to call anytime...*anytime*...she needed him.

"Or call if you'd just like to talk," he'd added with an appealing grin, as if he hoped she would telephone him for just that reason. She didn't, but sometimes she did look out her bedroom window and, from the lights she could see burning in his house, chart his evening activities as he moved from kitchen to living room to upstairs bedroom.

Although within a few days he, like the Gardiner household, was no longer sleeping in an upstairs bedroom. It was just too hot. Mr. Gardiner continued to occupy his first-floor bedroom, but everyone else slept on cots in the backyard. The legs of the cots were placed in water-filled cans to keep scorpions from crawling up to join the human occupants, and Gillian complained bitterly about this "primitive" Arizona life.

In the daily temperature of one-hundred-plus degrees, Beth gladly accepted Guy's offer of a ride to church on Sunday mornings. He also attended church with her, although it was, she suspected, more a part of his "watchdog" activities than a spiritual milestone. She was aware of those watchdog activities other times also, although he was discreet about them: a midday telephone call to check on her, a casual stop at the back door if he noticed an unfamiliar car parked at the Gardiner house; and once, on a hot, sleepless night, she'd even spied him taking a midnight stroll past the house.

After church, they also spent Sunday afternoons together, usually going to a popular swimming spot in a shallow irrigation canal. On Beth's Wednesday evenings off…which Gillian usually managed to sabotage with complaints about some devastating physical ailment brought on by the heat…they'd take the twins and Joey to play in a park or schoolground and eat a picnic supper of sandwiches that Guy put together in his kitchen.

Joey had his first birthday, an event celebrated with a cake made by Millie, the cook/housekeeper, and a little backyard party. It was bittersweet fun, with Guy and Beth delighting in their nephew but also thinking about Mark and Sylvia. Guy had a shower of presents for Joey, some appropriate, some he'd have to "grow into": a ball, a stick horse, a box of tin soldiers, a slate, a silver cup and spoon, a silly hat with a little propeller on top, and a half-dozen other items.

"When that man is a father, he's going to spoil his children dreadfully," Millie declared with a disapproving shake of her head, but she was also smiling fondly. Millie believed a big romance was brewing between "Annie" and Guy, even though Beth kept telling her they were just good friends.

Mrs. Dubuque brought her granddaughter over three mornings in a row. Beth made several sketches while the children played together in the backyard, but she did most of the actual painting late at night. She conscientiously did not want to steal time during what were her paid working hours. Even working under those limiting conditions, Beth finished the painting in less than two weeks, and Mrs. Dubuque was delighted with it. She insisted Beth come to her home when she formally unveiled the painting at a Saturday afternoon tea for a group of friends. Guy obligingly took care of the twins and Joey so Beth could go. From this meeting she received several requests to do other paintings, but she had to spread her commitments over a period of several months in the future because she knew there was a limit to how much of this Gillian would tolerate.

No more suspicious-looking hobos appeared, although once a young woman came to the door selling household products and seemed excessively curious about Joey and Beth. Beth mentioned it to Guy because he'd told her to report anything even slightly out of the ordinary to him. They were taking an evening stroll together, the twins dashing on ahead and Guy pushing Joey in the buggy. Sprinklers sparkled on lawns every-where, their spray creating welcome pockets of cool air in the breathless blanket of heat. Thunderclouds towered off to the southeast.

"Of course, there's nothing unusual about a door-to-door salesman," Beth said. "That it was a woman was a little out of the ordinary, but Millie said there have been a few lady sales-people before."

"But you say she seemed unusually curious about you and Joey."

"Yes, but that may have been because she was about my age and had a baby girl just a little younger than Joey. She hardly got to see the baby, she said, because she was out all day trying to sell her household supplies to make a living for the baby and herself and her widowed mother."

"A real sob story," Guy said skeptically. "Did you buy any-thing?"

"Some hand cream. It didn't cost much, but I thought it might help her out a bit. She looked so tired and discouraged. I also gave her a glass of lemonade."

Guy smiled. "You're a good woman, Miss Bethany Curtis. A

bit gullible, perhaps, but definitely good."

He leaned over and brushed Beth's temple with a kiss, a gesture more friendly and affectionate than romantic, but enough to fluster her. He'd never done anything like that before.

"You don't think her story was true?" she asked hastily to cover her feelings. "You think she may have been spying on me for your father?"

Guy tilted his head thoughtfully. He maneuvered the baby buggy expertly over a curb. "She was probably just what she said she was, a young woman struggling to make a living. But with a story continually rearranged to fit whatever she thought would win her the most sympathy and sales from a customer."

Beth laughed. "I probably was gullible, then. But I'm not sorry I bought her hand cream or gave her lemonade."

"Just out of curiosity, did you offer her a drink or did she ask for it?"

Beth hesitated, thinking back. "She said she was thirsty and asked if she could have a drink of water. When I went to the kitchen after it, she followed me."

"Uninvited?"

Beth hesitated again. "I'm not sure."

"Did she look around the house?"

"She didn't snoop, if that's what you mean. But my easel with a painting I'm working on was sitting in Mr. Gardiner's den…it's too hot to work upstairs…and she did notice that through the open door. But perhaps anyone would. I'm doing a portrait of a friend of Mrs. Dubuque's, and she wanted herself painted in the oddest purple dress."

Guy laughed. "Well, I don't think it's anything to worry about. But after this, if anyone comes to the door, no matter what the sob story is, just send them on their way, okay? Just to be safe."

They agreed to meet again the following evening, but that stroll never took place. Because by then Beth and Joey were no longer in Phoenix.

Fourteen

Guy's nerves prickled the moment he saw the folded paper tucked under the edge of the doorbell. It had not been a good day. A flat tire in the blistering sun. Walt rejecting Guy's suggestion for an in-depth article about a series of crimes frightening people in the Mexican area of town, scoffing, "Who cares what goes on over there? We don't have column space for that stuff." But he had plenty of space for a glowing account of a lodge award for Walt's hit-and-run buddy, City Councilman Cavanaugh.

Not a way to run a newspaper.

Even before Guy opened the note, he knew it must be bad news.

> *Guy,*
> *Gillian has decided she can't stand the heat here any*
> *longer, so we're all leaving immediately for Mr. Gardiner's*
> *ranch up in the mountains. I don't know how long we'll be*
> *away—at least several weeks, possibly all summer. I'll*
> *write you from there. Thanks for everything.*
> > *Annie*

The "A" in Annie looked bulgy, as if she'd started to sign *Beth* and thought better of it. Good idea. Anyone could have peeked and read it here on the door.

It wasn't really bad news, he assured himself as he opened the door of the hot, stuffy house. It was good that Beth and Joey could get out of the Phoenix heat, and they were probably safer from Nat at some isolated ranch than here.

Yet as he carried the note and a glass of ice water to the backyard, he couldn't escape experiencing an abandoned, letdown feeling. He and Beth had planned to attend a band concert Saturday evening. They were going to make homemade ice cream for Joey and the twins on Sunday afternoon.

Sitting in a lawn chair, he spread the note on his thigh and studied it. He liked Beth's handwriting, rounded and flowing without being pretentious or ornate. He lifted the sheet to his nose, but it carried none of her faint, feminine scent. It was, he thought unhappily, as impersonal as the words.

She could have telephoned him, he thought with a small rumble of resentment. She knew he had a phone on his desk now. If he'd had to leave town unexpectedly, he'd have wanted to hear *her* voice before he left. But obviously she'd felt no such need concerning him.

He reread each word, searching hopefully for some hidden meaning but finding none; it was simply a pleasant, courteous note.

It bore a great deal of resemblance, he thought slowly, to Beth's general attitude toward him. She was sweet and friendly; she held no grudges about the past and how he had threatened her and forced her to flee Ryman Springs. She trusted him where Joey was concerned; she'd proved that the time she left Joey in his care when she went to the unveiling of the painting at Mrs. Dubuque's home. She laughed with him; he was certain

157

she enjoyed his company.

But always there was a certain reserve about her. Both emotionally and physically, she kept him at arm's length. He'd sneaked one kiss on her temple, but she'd gently deflected any opportunity for a real kiss.

She was not, quite obviously, in love with him.

As he was with her.

He absorbed that full-fledged acknowledgment of love without surprise. He'd been falling in love with her from the first day he met her. Yet it was possible, he thought unhappily, that she let him hang around only because she knew he loved Joey, and she was too good and sweet and generous a person to deny him access to his nephew.

He slept late and skipped church that first Sunday after Beth and Joey went to the ranch. He'd spent many more Sunday mornings of his life out of church than in it, yet now the day felt oddly lacking, as if some essential part of it were missing. To keep busy he wandered down to the police station and spent the day listening to calls come in about car accidents and burglaries and a lost child. He followed police cars to the scene of a couple of minor crimes. But his main conclusion at the end of the day was that Beth out of sight was definitely not Beth out of mind.

He heard nothing from her the following week. Or the week after that. The silence both angered and worried him. He was strongly tempted to jump in the Packard and roar out to the ranch. Half of him wanted to take her in his arms and tell her he loved her. The other half wanted to yell at her for letting him stew about her safety and for not missing him the way he missed her.

The only reason he didn't rush out to the ranch was that he didn't know where it was. The Gardiner house was closed up tight. Even Walt the editor claimed he didn't know how to get in touch with Mr. Gardiner, which was probably true. Mr. Gardiner was very little involved in day-to-day management of the newspaper. A newspaper that actually, Guy observed, ran more smoothly without a tempestuous Gillian there throwing her weight around. Her former assistant had taken over as society editor, and Guy sometimes suspected she knew more about running the entire newspaper than anyone else.

On Wednesday of the following week Guy finally received a letter from Beth. He ran his fingers lightly over the envelope before opening it, feeling a little silly about his excitement and yet savoring the knowledge that he was touching something she had touched.

It was not a love letter, but it was pleasant and newsy. The higher-altitude temperatures were indeed cooler, and the scent of pines invigorating. She'd watched the branding of some cattle and been to a local rodeo. The twins were having a great time riding horses, gathering eggs in the henhouse, and playing in a nearby mountain pond. Joey, too, had been on a horse, held safely in the saddle in front of a cowboy, and Beth had also gone riding several times—tumbling off once when the horse made an unexpected turn. She included a cartoon of herself in an undignified sprawl on the ground, peering up at a very smug-looking horse. He laughed, delighted with the humorous little sketch, but missing her more every minute.

Beth still had no idea how long they would be staying at the ranch. Gillian had not said anything about leaving yet, but she was not too happy with ranch life. (A gentle understatement, Guy suspected, knowing Gillian's capacity for scorching complaints.) This was a working ranch, not set up to accommodate guests, and Gillian, Beth, the twins, and Joey were all crammed into one room. There was no telephone, and mail arrived or left only if someone happened to make the twenty-five mile drive into town, which didn't happen often.

So that explained the lack of telephone call or earlier letter from Beth, Guy realized. He should have known she was too thoughtful and considerate not to write or call if she could have.

Then his attention snapped back to an earlier word in the letter. *Cowboy*. He had an instant vision of someone lean and tanned and handsome riding a romantic, moonlit trail through the pines with Beth, flashing her a heart-stopping smile, sweet-talking her with an appealing cowboy drawl. His blood simmered as his mental moonlight silhouetted them by the mountain pond, arms entwined, faces hidden by the cowboy's ten-gallon hat.

The fact that a little further on in the letter Beth mentioned she was doing a painting of this same "picturesque old cowboy" made him feel a little better, but it didn't take away his disturbing picture of a whole crew of *other* young, lean, good-looking cowboys vying for Beth's attention.

Beth ended the letter saying that Mr. Gardiner and the housekeeper would be returning to Phoenix on Friday, and she'd try to send another letter with them. Her signature was again simply "Annie," with a P.S.: "Gillian is so bored that she's even having me do a painting of her!" And down in the left-hand corner was the tiny notation, "Isaiah 53:6."

Guy made up his mind instantly. He'd get directions to the ranch from Mr. Gardiner and ask for...no, *tell* Walt he was taking a few days off. He'd pick up a box of candy for Beth and get that cute little stuffed duck he'd seen in a downtown window for Joey.

Then, cowboys, stand back. Guy Wilkerson is taking over!

All day Thursday Guy felt like a kid awaiting a birthday party. Only one more day and he'd corner Mr. Gardiner for directions to the ranch!

That evening, as he did most evenings, he wandered down to the police station to see what was going on and wait for the unlikely chance to grab a scoop on some big crime story. It also helped pass the interminably slow-moving time until he could see Beth.

Lightning flickered off to the east as he drove through town, a ragged witches' brew of jagged streaks and flashes. He hoped there wouldn't be another storm like the one that had hit last week, with a blinding downpour that lasted less than an hour but filled the dry washes and low-lying streets with roaring, muddy water. He'd stared in astonishment at the sight of an old outhouse bobbing in the swirling flood that blocked his usual route home, two feet of water exploding through a dip which only that morning had looked as if it hadn't seen moisture since the days of Noah.

No rain penetrated the oppressive July heat as he lounged around the sweltering police station this night, however. Only a few calls came in: a domestic disturbance, a prowler who turned out to be an inebriated neighbor wandering into the wrong house, a vagrant who couldn't pay for a meal at a diner. He and the policemen told each other tired jokes: "Did you hear the one about the cop who was chasing a shoplifter, and it was so hot that they were both walking?" They spent a long time discussing the hypothetical question, "What would you do if you spotted John Dillinger walking down the street?"

By midnight Guy was ready to go home when a call came in from a woman who said she'd been watching a nearby house all week and something "very suspicious" was going on there.

With polite questioning, the officer drew out the information that this suspicious activity consisted of drawn window shades, a glimpse of a "sinister-looking" man, and large purchases of groceries by the lady of the house. Why she'd waited until the middle of the night to make this frantic call apparently hinged primarily on the fact that she couldn't sleep.

The sweating cop rolled his eyes as he put down the phone. "Deliver me from nervous women with overactive imaginations who see too many cops-and-robbers movies."

Guy laughed and lifted a hand in a goodbye wave. He didn't intend to tag along on the police investigation of the frivolous-sounding complaint, but when the police car headed in the same direction he was going he decided he may as well take a quick look on his way home.

Guy stopped the Packard a hundred feet behind the police car when it pulled up in front of a neat Victorian house, a cut above the others in the rundown area. The officers rang a door-bell, talked to a woman for several minutes, and then went on to a shabbier house with a dilapidated picket fence out front. The street was unpaved, potholed, and unlit except for an occasional dim glow of moonlight sliding through the shifting clouds overhead.

One of the officers knocked. After several minutes a porch light flicked on, and a frowzy woman in bathrobe and rag curlers opened the door. A nondescript mutt with tongue lolling out the side of its mouth offered the policemen a foot for a friendly paw-shake.

Guy smiled. Yep, a real suspicious situation here, folks. Big danger of being licked to death by a sloppy-tongued dog.

He drove slowly past the police car, looking for a good place to turn around because his headlights showed the street dead-ending in a tangle of cholla cactuses. He was thinking about seeing Beth, getting a long drink of iced tea when he got home, and wondering if he could find an all-night gas station so he could fill the tank tonight and not have to waste time doing it tomorrow.

He'd already turned into what he thought was an alley before he realized that, if it had ever been an alley, it wasn't one now. Now it was a cemetery of dead cars and dismembered car parts scattered like stray bones over dark patches of oil-soaked ground. He groaned as the axle crunched on something metallic.

He grabbed a flashlight from the glove compartment and got out to take a look. To his left was a leaning, open-sided shed that blocked his view of the police car on the street. Bits of junk littered the ground—rusty bolts, twists of coiled springs, shards of shattered glass. He knelt to peer under the Packard. He couldn't identify the lump jammed against the axle, but it didn't look as if the car was really wedged on top of it. Maybe if he just put the gearshift in reverse he could ease free. He stood, brushed sand and stickers off the knees of his trousers, turned off the flashlight, and opened the car door.

And felt a sudden cold prickle of apprehension, incongruous in the sultry night heat.

He paused, one hand on the door, the other clutching the flashlight.

Even as he mentally chided himself for imagination working overtime, his senses sharpened to a needle point at the palpable aura of lurking danger. His ears picked up the faint, intimate sounds of the hot night from windows open all up and down the street. He heard a toilet flushing. A ragged snore. A child's wail. A dark cloud covered the moon completely now, turning the buildings into featureless hulks. He smelled grease and oil, as if the shed were used for car repairs, and a faint stench of rotting garbage. The car door felt warm against his palm. The sudden shriek of an instant cat fight almost at his feet startled him, and he dropped the flashlight when a cat slammed into his leg.

Before he could straighten, something was on him. Something hot, heavy, muscular. An arm clamped around his chest, pinning his right arm against his side. Another arm wrapped around his left side, and then something sharp and metallic pressed against his throat.

"Don't make a sound," a harsh voice growled. "Not a whimper. Or you're dead."

Guy complied, blood hammering in his ears, throat instantly dry. He saw a dim flare of light and heard the faint murmur of voices from beyond the shed. The police must be searching the backyard of the picket-fenced house.

He felt the stubble of unshaven jaw against his ear, smelled the sour scent of beer breath. Tasted his own fear.

"This is what we're gonna do," the voice hissed in his ear. "Wait right here until the cops leave. Then you 'n' me are gonna drive out on the desert and I'll let you go. Got it?"

With the knife against his throat, Guy muttered a strangled, "Got it."

"You give me any trouble and I'll just kill you and take the car right now." Desperation filled every ruthless word.

They stood like two statues molded together, the man's thick chest a blockade of iron muscle against Guy's back. Guy's mind reeled crazily under the suddenness of the out-of-nowhere attack. One minute he was casually thinking about Beth and the next minute his life was on the line. Who was this man? He must have run out the back way when the police arrived at the house of the woman in the bathrobe.

Something trickled below the knife at his throat. Blood. Sweat. Both. His breath felt as if it stopped at the knife, unable to pass beyond the savage edge of steel to reach his lungs. His right arm numbed under the relentless grip binding it to his side.

Yet his mind blazed thoughts as fast and fiery as those earlier jagged bolts of lightning in the sky.

I can do nothing and be dead in a few hours. Because this guy was never going to let him remain alive once they were alone on the desert. Whoever he was, he was too desperate and ruthless to leave behind someone alive who could sic the authorities on him.

I can do something now and be dead in thirty seconds. Because one slash of the knife and his windpipe and jugular would be severed.

What do I do, God?

He could tell the attacker was bigger than he was, taller and heavier. Left-handed. Bull powerful. And with no inhibitions or conscience about murder, Guy felt certain.

The fighting cats suddenly zipped out from under the car in a tornado of fur and claws and screeches. The man cursed under his breath and lashed out at the cats with one foot, perhaps fearful the shrieking noise would draw the cops' attention.

Guy capitalized on the split-second opportunity provided and lashed out with his own foot, aware even as he did so that he might be slicing his outlook for life to zero.

His heel caught his attacker on the shin. Guy didn't wait for reaction to the first blow. He struck again, whipping his head backward against the solid jaw, seeing an explosion of black stars when skull met jawbone but recklessly throwing his weight to one side to unbalance his opponent.

They went down together in a tangle of arms and legs and curses. Guy landed on top, the crashing fall breaking the other man's hold on him, knife flashing a silvery arc as it rose and fell in a shaft of moonlight.

Guy scrambled away, hands frantically clawing the ground. The knife! Where was the knife! There!

A hulk lunged between Guy and the shifting moonlight. It landed on him like a truckload of dead meat. The crushing weight flattened him, and the knife flew out of his grip. The man laughed with evil glee, as if he enjoyed this deadly game. Beefy hands clamped around Guy's throat, and he knew his attacker needed no knife to kill. Fingers forced his neck forward; thumbs dug under his jaw and forced his head back. He tried to yell, but no sound escaped through the murderous clamp of flesh and bone around his throat. Yet even as his mind hung on the edge of oblivion, he knew another death would get him before strangulation finished him off. A broken neck. He could feel the vertebrae in his neck grating, grinding, crunching. Ten seconds to death now. Five—

His right hand uselessly flailed at the man's face, leaving no imprint on stubbled jaw or heavy nose or greasy hair. Incongruously he thought of Beth…Joey…Sylvia…God! He flung both hands outward, and his knuckles struck something hard and glassy. Frantically his fingers closed around the jagged shard of glass, but even as he grabbed it his mind registered it as a puny weapon against the ruthless mountain of muscle killing him. He could never lift his arm with enough strength to drive the dagger of glass into the hard muscles.

Yet with the last twitches of failing strength, the last echoes of fading determination, he forced every muscle and nerve to focus on one final, desperate effort. He clenched the splinter of glass, aimed it upward and drove it into the only vulnerable spot in the grinning face looming over him.

With a yelp of pain and fury the man let go and frantically grabbed at his face. He stumbled to his feet, dark blood streaming through his hands and over the stubble of whiskers. Guy, still on the ground, tried to rise, but his muscles wouldn't move; tried to scream but couldn't force sound through his tortured throat. But he didn't have to do either, because the man roared and staggered like a blinded, wounded bear, crashing into shed and machinery, screaming rage and pain, flinging blood in a hot arc.

The glare of a flashlight momentarily blinded Guy, and he flung a hand to his own eyes.

Confusion reigned. Yells. Lights. A peculiar ringing in Guy's ears. A weightlessness in his head as he lumbered to a sitting position. A blotting out of the outside world for a few frantic moments until breath finally streamed through his cramped throat into his crushed lungs.

By then the officers were leading the captured man out of the shed, his face bathed in blood, his roar now dissolved into helpless whimpers of pain. A crowd of people appeared out of nowhere. Someone made a frantic call for an ambulance. A dazed feeling of unexpected pity and regret flooded over Guy for what he'd had to do to this man to save himself.

He didn't realize until someone forced open his clenched fist that his hand was cut to the bone.

Fifteen

uy grumbled, but the doctor kept him in the hospital until Saturday morning. He had a stitched and bandaged right hand, numerous scratches and cuts, a tender lump on his head, and tape binding his cracked ribs. And even though his bruised body felt as sore as if it had been run through a printing press—he knew no one's role the other night had been more significant, or more personally costly, than his own—he didn't get to write the news story that made banner headlines on Friday afternoon's front page.

"Scotch" Wiseman got the byline about capture of the escapee from an East Coast prison, a convicted murderer neither the local nor eastern authorities had any idea was hiding with a distant cousin in the Phoenix area. The article played up the cleverness of the woman making the midnight telephone call and "alerting police to the suspicious situation," but Guy was negligently referred to as an "observer who happened to be on the scene" and who "unfortunately suffered minor injuries" during the apprehension. The escaped convict, although "seriously injured during the capture," was expected to be returned to the eastern prison after a few days under heavy guard in the local hospital. Guy was relieved that he hadn't fatally injured the man.

In spite of an amused annoyance with Scotch's downplaying of Guy's part in the capture, plus loss of the chance to write the big story, most of Guy's thoughts were elsewhere. On something so basic that he could only wonder that he'd so casually ignored it most of his life.

His train of thought ran like a repeating headline through his mind as he lay there sweating under a single sheet in the hospital room: What if he hadn't survived the assault? What if he'd died there on that oily ground amid the abandoned vehicles and discarded car parts? Was he ready to meet God? Had he anything to protect him from the judgment he deserved for all the wrongdoings in his life?

The answer was larger than any headline ever written: *NO!*

He'd vaguely contemplated death before. Who hadn't? Race-car driving was not for the weak of heart or nerve, and he'd sometimes steeled his nerves before a race by making frivolous jokes about death. Yet the possibility had never truly seemed real. Never before had he felt his life plunging out of control toward some bottomless pit; never before had he felt strength and awareness draining away. Never before had he come up against the raw fact that he was about to face the eternal God of the universe.

And someday, inevitably, it *would* happen. What then?

For a moment, as he listened to the clang and clatter of dinner trays in the hallway and watched a deliveryman hurry past the door with a florist's ornate bouquet, he felt a peculiar sense of amazement that people were going about their ordinary lives so unconcerned about what was coming, blindly existing for the moment, living as if they would never have to meet their Lord.

Immediately he chided himself for being morbid. He was simply having what was no doubt a common reaction to a life-threatening experience. He rang the bell and asked for a pill so he wouldn't lie awake all night thinking such depressing and disturbing thoughts.

Just before the hospital released him on Saturday, a nurse brought an unexpected message that Walt had phoned and told him to take a few days off to recuperate. One of the policemen had kindly moved the Packard to the hospital's parking lot for him. Guy's plan was to jump in the car, find out from Mr. Gardiner how to reach the ranch, and leave immediately.

His first realization, after a shaky hobble to the car, was that he was in no condition to *jump* anywhere. His head no longer throbbed, but sitting in the car returned the ache to his ribs. And, after trying to steer and shift gears with a bandaged hand as cumbersome as a birdcage attached to his arm, he doubted he could manage a long drive.

As a final barrier to his plans to see Beth he also found, when he walked over to the Gardiner house, that Mr. Gardiner and the housekeeper had not returned from the ranch on Friday after all.

So here he was, alone on this hot summer night, sweating on a cot in the backyard. Overhead, the radiance of a silver-white moon dimmed the nearby stars, but farther out they glittered like sprinkles of diamond dust. Guy didn't intend to think about God and his nebulous relationship with him on this night; he simply intended to sleep.

But it was not possible, he thought almost grumpily, to lie under such a display of moon and stars and *not* contemplate the creator of such magnificence. The words of Genesis almost seemed to ring in his ears: *And God made two great lights…the lesser light to rule the night; he made the stars also.*

God. There he was, back in Guy's thoughts again. Although in truth, Guy had to admit, God hadn't really been *out* of his thoughts since that moment he dangled over the pit of death.

Okay, he thought a little resentfully, he'd think about God. Although maybe it was a little late. After all, he'd had one chance with God, through Mrs. Sommersby's loving teaching and guidance, and he'd carelessly let it slip away. Why should God give him another chance?

Yet God hadn't demanded his presence there on that oily patch of ground, with a murderer's hands around his throat. Instead God had put a shard of glass within his desperate reach...

For no particular reason he thought of that Bible reference Beth had scribbled in the corner of her letter, almost as if it were an afterthought. Isaiah something. Maybe he'd look it up tomorrow.

And what if his life were required of him tonight? Another of those ridiculous, morbid thoughts, he scoffed instantly. He was lying here in his own backyard, safe in bed. Yet he'd had no thought that other night, either, when making the casual decision to follow the police car, of the precariousness of his life's perch at that moment.

And, like it or not, he had to admit, looking death in the eye changes your perspective.

He got out of bed and trudged inside. Beth's letter was on top of the bureau. He tilted the page to read the tiny notation in the corner. Isaiah 53:6. He got out his Bible and located the reference, aware that he had been foraging in the gilt-edged pages enough recently that he did know where Isaiah was located.

"All we like sheep have gone astray; we have turned every one to his own way; and the Lord hath laid on him the iniquity of us all."

Oh, yes, that was him. Gone astray like some wandering sheep. Yet the words didn't go on to say, "Okay, you had your chance and you walked away, so don't bother me now." Instead, Jesus had taken on himself the "iniquity of us all."

And that includes *you,* Guy Wilkerson. *Your* iniquity. It came to him as it hadn't before, like a blank wall transforming into a window and letting in the light, that this was what the faithful had when they faced death, the knowledge that the sacrifice of Jesus protected them from condemnation for all the times they had done wrong or fallen short of doing right.

He'd heard it in Pastor Merriman's sermons; he'd stumbled across it in his browsings through the Bible. Yet only now did it suddenly become personal and *real.* Almost frantically his fingers scrambled to find a remembered reference from one of the pastor's recent sermons. John something…Yes, there it was: John 5:24. "He that heareth my word, and believeth on him that sent me, hath everlasting life, and shall not come into condemnation; but is passed from death unto life."

There it was, the wonderful promise, the breathtaking assurance, the eternal haven of safety.

Like a man hungry for something more than food, he read voraciously for hours, the words now illuminated by a glowing spotlight of truth and meaning.

And finally he knelt beside the chair, giving his heart and life to the Lord, basking in the salvation offered through Jesus' sacrifice, thanking and praising and loving. By the time he rose from the floor he felt stiff and weary physically, but cleansed and reborn spiritually.

He stretched out on the cot again, his good hand under his head and his bandaged hand a clumsy lump resting on his chest, as he once again contemplated the grandeur of the Lord's handiwork spread overhead. A faint paling in the eastern sky signaled the coming of dawn.

Was this why you put me there on the ground, Lord, under a countdown to death, so I'd finally see the light?

Amazingly, in spite of his weariness, Guy began to laugh. Laughter of joy, laughter of appreciation, laughter of communion with such a loving God. Because he could almost hear the Lord say, *I knew it was going to take more than a pep talk to make a man as stubborn and hard-headed as you see the light, Guy Wilkerson.*

Yes, indeed. Much more than a pep talk. He'd nearly had to be blinded by the brilliance of the light before he saw it. Then the laughter faded into seriousness, to an awed acknowledgment of the magnitude of what had just happened. Because he now knew he could meet God without fear or dread when that inevitable time came. Meet him not as some noble or righteous person who had lived a perfect life but as one forgiven, covered by the sacrifice Jesus had made.

Beth tilted her face closer to the open window, seeking to catch a cooling breeze from the moving car, but the desert heat was like sticking her head into an open oven. The heat shimmered in waves, distorting the distant mountains and making the road ahead look as if it disappeared into a lake that she knew couldn't be there. A dusty haze hung over the city in the distance.

Mr. Gardiner and the housekeeper were supposed to have returned to Phoenix over a week ago, but he'd hurt his back in a spill from a horse and wound up bedridden for several days. Now Mr. Gardiner, the housekeeper, and Adrian rode in the lead car, and Gillian, Beth, Ariana, and Joey followed behind. Gillian, who had complained about the heat before they left

Phoenix, and then complained about the isolation and bore-
dom of the ranch, was now back to condemning the heat.

"I don't know how anyone can live here in the summer," she
gasped melodramatically as she fanned herself with one hand.

Beth had mixed feelings about returning to the city. The valley
heat was indeed excessive, but she was less affected by it than
Gillian was. She was looking forward to fulfilling her painting
commitments…and seeing Guy again.

Yet she also felt a certain apprehension about seeing Guy.
Not because she feared him; she'd lost all suspicion he'd betray
her and Joey to his father. It was more that she was uneasy
about the relationship between herself and Guy; when she'd left
Phoenix so unexpectedly she'd had the feeling that their being
separated for a while was probably a good thing, that a "cooling
off" in something more than the desert temperature was needed.

They reached the house about dusk. Mr. Gardiner immediately started making telephone calls neglected over the past
weeks. Gillian played wilting princess and dramatically
announced she must have a cooling bath before the heat over-
came her. Millie and Beth started airing out the stuffy house
and unloading the cars, at the same time answering Gillian's
various demands yelled from the bathroom. The twins chased
around like small explorers revisiting old territory, squealing
when they discovered some forgotten treasure. Joey toddled
behind as best he could but occasionally plopped down, howling when he was left behind.

Into the midst of this chaos, while Beth was searching the
car for a "cucumber creme" lotion that Gillian insisted must
have spilled out of her bag, came a new voice.

"Beth? I mean, Annie, is that you?"

Beth popped out of the car rump first, auburn hair
disheveled, face flushed, and dress twisted sideways.

"It *is* you!"

Before Beth could scarcely think what was happening, Guy swept her up in his arms and whirled her around until her feet flew out as if she were on some wild carousel. Then he planted her on the ground and kissed her so thoroughly that she had to cling to him dizzily. He didn't let her go, but his mouth finally lifted from hers, and she shook her head to gather her blurred image of several grinning faces into one.

But before she could say anything, he stepped back, shoulders hunched, one hand clutching his ribs. "Maybe I shouldn't have done that," he gasped ruefully.

Only then did she see his other hand, the fingers protruding from a bandage wrapped around palm, knuckles, and wrist. "Guy, what happened to you!"

"Would you believe I helped capture a desperate prison escapee?"

She surveyed him carefully, noting his short, quick breathing. "I might."

"I'll tell you all about it later, then. Right now, I'm just too happy to see you! Oh, Beth, have you any idea how much I've missed you?" He ran his hand along the nape of her neck, where her hair was finally growing to a semblance of feminine length, as if to make certain she was really there, solid and real, not some figment of his imagination. He kissed her again, on forehead and cheeks and tip of nose.

Beth wanted him to stop...and didn't want him to stop.

The twins dashed by in another whirlwind of exploration, but Joey's plump legs were giving out and he stopped to clutch Beth's leg with both hands. Guy started to swoop him up but apparently thought better of it. Instead he leaned over and planted a kiss on top the blond head. Joey, ever affectionate, returned the kiss and then toddled off again.

"Do you think he remembers me?" Guy sounded a bit wistful, as if he had been separated from Joey for months rather than a few weeks.

Before Beth could answer, Joey had taken a tumble, this one accompanied by tears and cries.

"I think he's saying Mama!" Guy said in amazement. "When did he start doing that?"

Beth laughed as she scooped up the little boy who was so tired but refusing to give in to it. "I'm not sure. Somehow I thought there would be a definite moment when a child said a first word, and you could write down the date and remember it forever. But with Joey it's been more like sounds that slip back and forth between babble and something understandable." She laughed again. "Or maybe we hear what we want to hear. The twins insist that something that sounds like 'Ree' is Ariana, and 'Aid' is Adrian."

Beth put Joey down to sleep in the shade of the car, doors wide open to catch the breeze, a spot that was cooler than the hot house. They still had to get the cots set up outside for the night.

She knew she should be doing that, but when Guy took her hands in his she didn't pull away. They studied each other without saying anything, and he grinned again, as if the happy smile muscles had total control of his face. Then, still without speaking, he leaned over and kissed her once more, a kiss full on the mouth. She just stood there, eyes closed, thinking she shouldn't be allowing this, and yet absurdly wanting to fling her arms around him and go right on kissing him.

"We have a lot to talk about," he said finally, with an emotional huskiness in his voice.

"Yes, we do," she agreed brightly, deliberately giving his words a non-intimate interpretation. This was why she'd been uneasy about returning to Phoenix. "Northern Arizona is beautiful, and the ranch—"

He smiled as if he knew what she was doing. "I want to tell you what happened to me while you were gone."

"Yes, I want to hear all about your wild adventure with the prison escapee."

"It's more than that. Much more."

He was looking at her with such loving tenderness that Beth's heart turned a panicky flip-flop. But just then a frazzled Millie dashed out with Gillian's demand that if Beth couldn't find the cucumber creme she wanted her other apricot lotion. Immediately.

Beth smiled, grateful for the interruption. "The princess calls."

"What I have in mind is that you tell the princess to go jump in the lake...or whatever the equivalent term may be here in the desert," he said with sudden fierceness. "And then come marry me."

At Beth's shocked expression...she'd half expected this, but not quite so bluntly!...he tilted his head and smiled. "Sorry. I didn't intend to come out with that so soon. Pretend I didn't mention it, okay?"

"Okay," she agreed shakily.

"Do you want to go to church tomorrow morning?"

"Oh, yes." She hadn't been to church since leaving Phoenix. She'd communed with the Lord regularly through prayer and her Bible, but it wasn't the same as being in his house.

"Okay. I'll pick you up at the usual time."

And then he firmly gathered her in his arms and kissed her once more.

Sixteen

❧

Guy heard Pastor Merriman's sermon, but his thoughts were on what was coming next. When the invitation came, he jumped to his feet and eagerly strode down the aisle to make his public commitment to the Lord. Now he knew why others he'd seen do this were both smiling and tearful!

His eyes sought Beth's as he faced the congregation. She smiled and nodded agreement when he spoke a few words about his newfound faith, but he was surprised and puzzled by a shadow of something less than wholehearted approval behind the smile.

Afterward there were hugs and handshakes and welcoming words, so many that it wasn't until Guy and Beth were driving home, Joey in Beth's lap and the twins in the backseat, that Beth's silence made obvious the fact that something was troubling her. Guy waited until the twins had tumbled out of the car and rushed into the house to get out of their Sunday-best clothes before saying anything. He stretched his arm across the back of the car seat, fingers lightly touching Beth's shoulder.

"Beth, is something wrong? You don't seem particularly

pleased about my decision for the Lord."

She turned her head to look at him. "Of course I'm pleased! I've hoped and prayed for this."

He grinned. "Then how about a little more enthusiasm? Maybe a few handsprings and cartwheels of joy! Instead you look as glum as if one of your paintings had just crashed into a bucket of mustard."

Beth smiled and smoothed a rebellious cowlick of Joey's hair. He decided to clamber into the backseat, and she let him go. "I'm sorry. I don't mean to look glum. It's just that—"

"I knew there was a 'it's just that.' So what is it?"

"Last night you asked me to marry you—" She broke off and blushed lightly. "Well, you suggested it and then you took back the suggestion, so perhaps that doesn't qualify as an official proposal—"

"I'll make it official, right now, if you won't again look as horrified as if I'd just suggested robbing a local bank."

"I did not look horrified!" Beth objected indignantly. "I was simply…surprised, that's all."

"Surprised?" he scoffed good-humoredly. "Anyone with powers of observation any more acute than those of a stump could see I've been falling in love with you. And I know there's nothing wrong with your powers of observation."

"Yes, I've known," she admitted.

"But you don't feel the same way about me."

"Guy, I think it's wonderful if you truly did find the Lord again—"

"The important words here are *if* and *truly?*"

"I have the uneasy feeling that you perhaps did this as…" She hesitated and then stumbled ahead as if feeling her way through a spiky maze. "I mean, I don't think you were necessarily *insincere*, but perhaps, in a burst of impulsive enthusiasm…"

"The same enthusiasm with which I picked you up and whirled you around and kissed you when I hadn't seen you for several weeks?"

"Something like that."

"You think I came forward this morning to gain your approval. As a ploy to get you to marry me."

She laughed ruefully. "It sounds terribly egotistical when you put it in those blunt words. As if I think I'm some sort of irresistible *femme fatale,* and any man would jump through hoops to have me." She put her head down and shook it as if embarrassed.

Guy cupped his hand under her chin and forced her to look at him. "Beth, I love you and I suppose I would jump through hoops or climb mountains or swim rivers for you, and I do hope you approve of my acceptance of Jesus as my Savior. But it really has nothing to do with you. This is between the Lord and me. And I didn't make some last-minute, impulsive decision to go forward this morning. This was simply the public statement of what already happened to me in private. You remember that Bible reference you scribbled in the corner of your letter?"

"Bible reference?"

"Isaiah 53:6. About sheep going astray."

She hesitated a moment as if sifting this through a file of verses in her head, then nodded recognition. "But I don't remember putting it in the letter."

God working in his mysterious ways again, Guy thought. But he didn't comment on that. Instead he told her about what had happened to him there on the ground in that oily cemetery of abandoned car parts, with a murderer's hands around his throat, and how it had changed everything between himself and the Lord.

Beth touched his cheek. "Oh, Guy, I had no idea… Are you all right?" Her blue eyes searched his face with tender concern.

"Outside of stitches from my fingertips to my elbow, a throat undoubtedly scarred for life and thirty-six broken ribs…"

He smiled, and Beth laughed at his melodramatic exaggeration. "I'm sure I'd believe you if it weren't that I'm reasonably certain a man doesn't have thirty-six ribs."

"I should have known better than to try to work on your sympathies," he grumbled.

Beth lifted his bandaged hand and with a mischievous smile kissed each exposed fingertip. "How's that for sympathy? All better now?" He grinned, but her voice turned serious. "*Are* you okay?"

"My ribs are still sore," he admitted. "The doctor said a couple of them are cracked. But I'm fine. All I have to do is keep the ribs taped for a while, and go back to have the stitches removed from my hand in a few days. But I'm changed, Beth. Truly."

"I'm glad, Guy. So very glad." Impulsively she leaned over and kissed him on the cheek.

"But I certainly don't expect you to marry me *because* of this. If you marry me, I want it to be because you love me, as I love you."

"And if I won't marry you?" she challenged lightly.

Guy swallowed. He hadn't really let himself think much about that possibility. But when he did force himself to do so now, he felt it like a dark cloud of pain looming on his emotional horizon, a pain so threatening he couldn't even bring himself to make light of or tease about it. "I'll be sorry, Beth. Very sorry," he said huskily. "But it won't change my relationship with God."

She nodded slowly, as if that satisfied some question in her mind.

"All I'm asking, at this point," he added, "is that you give marrying me some honest thought and consideration."

Beth had no problem doing that. Actually, she had an unusual amount of time for herself and thinking. Gillian's interest in being a society editor had apparently faded, and she didn't go back to the newspaper after their return home. To Beth's surprise, Gillian actually started acting more like a mother, taking the twins to a friend's private pool to swim, supervising their baths, and reading to them at bedtime. Sometimes she also took them to inappropriate movies or let them eat too much ice cream, but she did appear to be making a more serious effort at motherhood. Beth also thought there must be a new man in Gillian's life, because Gillian often spent time in her room with the door shut, her voice an intimate murmur on the phone, but, oddly, he never made an in-person appearance.

With her free time, Beth painted, enjoyed Joey's newfound fascination with word sounds...and thought about Guy.

She wasn't ready to give him the answer he wanted, but with his acceptance of the Lord she knew an invisible barrier between them had been removed.

They saw each other every day—casual, companionable get-togethers rather than formal dates. They cooked dinner at his house and enjoyed Joey's delight at toddling through the sprinkler in the backyard. Or sometimes Guy came to the Gardiners' backyard and watched her paint. He made her laugh with lively tales about behind-the-headlines details from the newspaper, but they also had serious discussions about deep spiritual matters. And once they talked about Nat Wilkerson. Although there had been no more suspicious incidents, or at least, as Guy pointed out reluctantly, none they recognized as being suspicious, neither was convinced Nat had abandoned his arrogant belief that Joey belonged to him.

Guy kissed her lightly a few times but she knew he was carefully holding back on the fervor and exuberance of those first welcome-home kisses. She appreciated him not crowding her, either physically or emotionally.

And, taking her time, she quickly knew the affection she'd been careful to keep under reserved control in the past was now burgeoning like some rampant wildflower. She felt the wild bloom of love at the most diverse of times: when Guy roughhoused with Joey on the lawn, and when he raged passionately about his frustrations with the way the newspaper was run; when he kissed her on the nape while she peeled potatoes at his kitchen sink, and when he held her hand and gave her a proud and loving glance as they walked into church together.

Yet she wasn't about to rush too soon into anything as vital and permanent as marriage. There was plenty of time.

Then Gillian issued her bombshell announcement.

Seventeen

Guy dashed into the street with a coat to shelter Beth from the sudden downpour, but it was already too late. She was drenched, her body curved protectively over a giggling Joey.

"Hey, aren't kids supposed to be scared of thunder and storms?" Guy chided his nephew with mock severity. He wrapped the coat around Joey and slung him over his shoulder in the sack-of-flour way Joey loved.

"He thinks it's all great fun, and he wants to be out playing in it." Beth laughed and wiped at the water streaming down her cheeks. "When I left the house two minutes ago it wasn't even sprinkling." She held up a hand. "Now this."

They dashed to the shelter of the porch and watched the brief but savage onslaught of summer storm while thunder rumbled overhead. Off to the south the sky was a clear, tranquil blue.

Beth's dress clung like a wet glove to her body, and her shoes squished. Her hair, usually styled in a soft curl now that it had grown out of the rough boyish cut, was glued to her head. Yet, with good-natured laughter dancing in her blue eyes, the auburn of her wet hair gleaming, and the sheer goodness of her a golden aura reaching out to envelop him, Guy had never found her more appealing.

She flicked a drop of water off his nose. "Don't stare at me! I feel like a wet spaniel dragged out of an irrigation ditch."

"You've never looked more beautiful." Guy dumped Joey on the porch floor. "And I love you."

But Beth turned to look down the street at the Gardiner house with a troubled expression. "Gillian and her former husband have decided to reconcile. She and the twins are moving back to Boston. She's asked me to come with them."

"I guess I'm—"

"Flabbergasted?" Beth filled in. "That was my first reaction."

"Are you considering her offer?"

"She's promised a raise, and I'd have every Sunday and one weekday off, so I could paint or take art classes or do whatever I wanted."

Guy listened with dismay to these attractive enticements. Rather than rush in with arguments or persuasions, he carefully asked a neutral question. "How did this come about?"

"Gillian has been on the telephone with him almost daily since we returned from the ranch. I'm afraid she may be reconciling with him mostly because she's dissatisfied with life here," Beth added, "but I'm praying that it will work for them. The twins need their father, and I doubt he's as despicable as she's made him out to be."

"Have you made a decision?" Guy asked, suddenly afraid Beth had already gone beyond just considering the offer.

"If I don't go, I'll be out of a job when they leave."

Guy remained silent as long as he could, which he guessed was all of three seconds. Then he abandoned nice-guy neutrality and fiercely said what was in his heart. "Don't go, Beth. Stay here. Marry me."

Water still dripped from her hair, and she squeezed a wet lock with one hand. "I see...some things to be concerned about."

"And I see God's hand in this! He knows his people sometimes need a push to get them moving, and this is your shove toward marrying me."

Beth smiled. "Maybe it's a shove toward *not* marrying you. His way of putting a couple of thousand miles between us," she suggested.

Guy braced a foot on the porch railing. The quick downpour had already gentled to a patter that would be over in a few minutes. What she suggested could be true, he agreed reluctantly. But until God made his opposition clear, he intended to do everything he could to persuade Beth to be his wife.

"Beth, I love you. I think you love me. We both love the Lord. So what are these 'concerns'?"

"It's one big concern," Beth said slowly. Guy followed her gaze as Joey gleefully splashed in a puddle of rainwater on the top step. "What you did interrupted your father's plan to get Joey, and other problems may have detoured his plans temporarily. But I don't think he's permanently given up on taking Joey away from me."

Guy nodded agreement. "When Nat makes up his mind to do something, he's a hard man to stop." Offhand, Guy couldn't think of any situation in which his father had come out the permanent loser.

No, that wasn't true. He may have won on his ruthless business deals, may shrewdly have risen in wealth and status, but he'd lost with Sylvia. Sylvia had God on her side.

"So what do we do when he comes after us again?" Beth asked. "Do the three of us pick up and run and hide? Can we live like that, always looking over our shoulders?"

Guy wrapped his hands around Beth's arms. "I've thought

about this, and we aren't going to run, not ever. We stand. And we fight."

"How?" she asked bluntly.

"The first thing we do is get married. Then we immediately start adoption proceedings to make Joey legally ours. We also come out of hiding. We let Nat know where we are, what we're doing, and that we're both in the battle now. That it's no longer Wilkerson money and power against a lone woman."

"But he has so much money and power."

"With the two of us eager and able to give Joey a normal, loving home, I don't think Nat can take him away from us. And there's another weapon I plan to add to our arsenal. I'm going to buy the newspaper. The only reason Mr. Gardiner kept the *Courier* when he first got it was because Gillian wanted to be a society editor. Now, from a tentative conversation I had with him, I think he'll be happy to sell."

"You're going to fight your father with words?" Beth sounded doubtful.

"Words are more powerful than you might think. Knowing that whatever he does will hit the newspapers will be a threat Nat can't ignore. He'll also know I can put an intense and unfavorable spotlight on things he's already done. I can cause him big trouble."

"But we're in Phoenix and he's in St. Louis."

"I think St. Louis newspapers will be very interested in what a Phoenix newspaperman has to say about one of their more important citizens. But that isn't the only reason I want the newspaper, of course. I see so much that could be done with it! Bringing out the problems of Indians in this state, which are totally ignored now. Addressing water usage. Phoenix uses water as if the supply were inexhaustible." He waved a hand at the sprinklers churning merrily on lawns all up and down the street, in an effort to duplicate a scene and style of life from some totally different climate. "But the water isn't inexhaustible, and we need to start thinking about that now. And then there's the little matter of concealing from public scrutiny what some of our elected officials are doing."

He paused and laughed a little self-consciously. "I guess I jumped on my soapbox there, didn't I?"

"It's a soapbox you can be proud of."

"So, does that take care of your concerns?"

A little awkwardly she asked, "Can you do this…financially?"

"Things may be tight for a while." He smiled. "I won't be able to shower you with jewels and fur coats immediately."

"And I'm in desperate need of several fur coats, of course, here in the desert!"

"I'll have to sell some assets to swing it. But one way or another, yes, I can manage it financially."

"I can help," she offered. "I have several commissions for paintings lined up. Perhaps I can even find a gallery that will carry my work."

Guy looked at her, and she looked at him as they both digested what she had just said. It wasn't the financial offer that interested Guy, much as he appreciated it.

"Do I hear a *yes* to my proposal in there somewhere?"

Beth blinked as if she had perhaps surprised herself, then added with a tremulous smile, "I believe you do."

"Do you love me, Beth?"

"Yes."

His heart thundered at the sweet simplicity of that declaration which came without hesitation or qualifications or conditions. He put his arms around her, looked into her eyes for a long moment, and kissed her with all the love that was in his own hammering heart.

Then he lifted his head and looked into her eyes again. "I love you, Beth. I started loving you almost the day I met you, and I'll never stop. And you know I love Joey, too."

He kissed her again, gently and tenderly, but with the sweet stirrings of passion. "How soon can we get married?" he demanded huskily. "Tomorrow? *Today?*"

Beth laughed at his bold eagerness. She draped her arms around his neck and ran her fingers through the thick bronze-gold of his hair. "Today is definitely out of the question. And tomorrow is also rushing things a bit. I feel obligated to stay with Gillian and the twins until they move back East. How about the week after they leave?"

Guy pulled a long face at the delay, then grinned. "If I come over and help with packing, maybe we can get them out by day after tomorrow?"

"I thought modern men were adverse to marriage," she teased lightly. "That women practically had to drag them into it."

"Not a man who is as much in love as I am."

Again he gathered her into his arms, intent on showing her that love, but Joey, with a small-boy lack of concern for the niceties of a romantic moment, suddenly wiped his wet hands on Guy's trouser leg.

They both laughed, but Beth's laughter faded into a shaky question.

"Guy, what if your father's determination to get Joey doesn't take a…legal path? What if he does what you warned me from the very first he was capable of doing, and simply steals Joey?"

"I think, once he realizes the two of us are in this together, he won't dare try anything like that. But we'll move as soon as possible to a house and yard that are more secure than this one. If the worst did happen, and Nat somehow managed to snatch

Joey in spite of all our precautions, as our legally adopted child we'd have the ammunition to get him back."

Beth nodded, reassured. "Yes, that's true."

But getting the security of a legal adoption could take considerable time, Guy had to admit to himself. Time in which Nat might still arrogantly try to carry out some underhanded scheme.

"I'll take care of you and Joey, I promise," he vowed. "You'll be safe with me."

Silently he strengthened that vow, fiercely adding a provision that he suspected might be too harsh or severe for Beth to accept if she knew it.

Nat isn't going to get Joey, Beth. Not legally or any other way. I'll never let Nat or any of his henchmen hurt either of you. And if that means my life...or someone else's...so be it.

On the drive to church the following Sunday Guy told Beth he'd made a deal with Mr. Gardiner for the newspaper, part cash and part trade of a St. Louis property. Guy would be taking over management of the newspaper in less than a month.

He grinned. "Which allows just enough time for a wedding and honeymoon."

"Honeymoon!" Beth echoed. She had thought as far ahead as planning a small wedding ceremony. She loved Guy and looked forward to family life with him and Joey. She vaguely pictured another child or two sometime in the future. But the possibility of an actual honeymoon had not occurred to her. She felt herself blushing lightly at the suggestion of intimacy the word engendered.

"I thought a few days in San Francisco would be nice. We could take the train and stay in a good hotel. Enjoy room service and breakfast in bed."

More visions of intimacy! "Yes, that would be...lovely," she echoed faintly.

Guy looked at her sharply. "Hey, you're not thinking about backing out, are you?" Before she could reply he braked and swung the car sharply to the curb. "I intended to do this in a more romantic setting, with flowers and candlelight, but I think the time to put an official stamp on this engagement is right now."

Beth felt alarmed, uncertain what he intended. "We'll be late for church—"

"God will understand. Close your eyes," he commanded.

Beth did so with reluctance, feeling vulnerable with people on their way to church passing by and peering at them curiously.

"Tighter!" Guy commanded. "You're peeking."

Beth squeezed her eyelids shut harder, unconsciously squeezing her fists shut at the same time. First she felt Guy prying the left one open, and then there was the smooth glide of something metallic on her ring finger. She opened her eyes to the dazzle of a diamond flanked by two pairs of smaller stones.

"Guy, it's beautiful!" She laughed breathlessly as the stone caught the sunlight and zigzagged a flash of brilliance with the tremble of her hand. The flash attracted Joey's attention, and he oohed and fingered the ring curiously. "I...don't know what to say!"

"Just tell me Gillian is leaving, so we can get on with the wedding and I can slip the matching wedding band on your hand." He grinned mischievously. "And so we can get on with the honeymoon."

After church Guy said he had something he wanted to show her.

They drove out of town, heading northeast, and Beth

assumed he'd discovered some scenic new viewpoint or perhaps a hidden oasis for a picnic. Instead, the dusty lane wound leisurely through the summer-baked hills, finally coming to an old wooden gate flanked by two majestic saguaros.

"What is this?"

"You'll see."

What Beth saw after they drove through the pole gate was an adobe house, the same color as the enormous, pinkish-tan boulders beyond it, and looking almost as much a part of the desert as they did. The house was low, one story, square as a fort, plain, and yet there was an appealing grace to the gentle curve of the top line of the front wall. No water-hungry green grass and eastern trees surrounded this house; instead, a variety of cactus, rocks, and native palo verde and mesquite created a natural garden of desert beauty. The house was obviously unoccupied, but an air of gentle waiting, more than abandonment, hung over it.

"What a lovely old place!"

"It's the main house of what was once a big ranch, although only a few acres remain now." Guy opened the carved wooden door with an ornate iron key and led Beth inside, where adobe walls two feet thick kept the interior comfortably cool even in the heat of this late August day. The bare interior smelled unused, dry, and dusty, but it was not an unpleasant scent.

"Whose is it? Won't they mind our snooping?"

They wandered through a living room with exposed wooden beams overhead and the blackened cavern of a fireplace; massive bookshelves still laddered the walls of a den; sunlight flared brilliant squares of light in the deeply recessed windows. Empty flowerpots stood at a kitchen window, as if hopefully waiting for someone to fill them.

Beth twined her fingers together as she peered into a large

room on the north side. What a wonderful spot for an easel! The opposite wing of the square had a row of rooms that her imagination immediately turned into a master bedroom and a nursery, plus individual bedrooms for a family of children as they grew older. All the rooms were bare except for an enormous dark table in the dining room…big as a tennis court was her first impression!…and the skeleton of an equally enormous, hand-carved wooden bed in the bedroom.

In the center of it all lazed a courtyard paved with graceful swirls of sunbaked brick. A trio of sturdy, gold-green palo verde trees threw an intricate pattern of shade on the bricks. In the center stood a huge old iron bell hung on a heavy timber, perhaps the relic of some long-ago mission.

"You're thinking of this for us?" Beth asked tentatively.

"A Linotype operator at the newspaper told me about it. It's part of an estate with numerous heirs, of which he's one, and about the only thing they agree on is that they want to get rid of this place. The price is very reasonable, but it would take a lot of work to bring it up to modern standards…"

He glanced around as if searching for some favorable point to bring to her attention. They were now back in the long living room that stretched the full width of the house. Their footprints looked like a jumble of modern petroglyphs on the dusty floor. Dust covered Joey's diaper, from when he'd dragged his little bottom on the floor.

"I know it's a bit primitive…" Guy paused uncertainly, then took a deep breath. "Because of buying the newspaper we'll also be short on funds for a while and may not immediately be able to afford to do everything that needs to be done to it."

Yes, the house *was* primitive, and much needed doing. The lone bathroom had been semi-modernized, but the big place needed at least two more. The kitchen was so old-fashioned that a pioneer wife would undoubtedly feel right at home in it. Weeds thrust dry stalks through cracks between the bricks in the courtyard, every one of them as stickery and thorny as only desert weeds can be. Small piles of sticks and bits of cactus in corners of several rooms showed the presence of some small, industrious intruders. Shards of shattered glass littered the floor near a broken window. Their tromping around had raised so much dust that Beth suddenly went into a string of sneezes.

"Have you put any money on it yet?" she managed to say between sneezes. "Signed any papers?"

Guy shook his head, his expression more resigned than disappointed. "No, I wouldn't do that without consulting you first."

She sneezed again. "Then sign them, quick, before someone snatches it out from under us!"

His face lit up, and he grabbed her arms. "You mean that? You're not just trying to be a good sport?"

The idea of renovating the place was intimidating; Beth could imagine Gillian fleeing from it in horror. It would take time, especially if money was short. But she'd seen electric poles only a mile away, so electricity could be brought in much more easily than to many rural homes. The house was big and cool, as strong and solid as if it were a part of the earth itself, and every outside window opened onto a lovely desert scene. There was a wonderful feeling of being surrounded by ties to the past; a place where people had lived and loved and no doubt died as well, because it was a place a person could call home for a lifetime. It was also secure as a fortress, with the central courtyard protected by the rooms around it, and the dusty road billowing a giveaway flag of dust at the approach of any car. Here Joey would be safe from whatever scheme Nat hatched to snatch him.

Beth felt as if she'd been on a long, wandering journey most of her life, and now she'd found home. "Oh, yes, I'm sure."

Guy kissed her, a kiss filled with passion and promise and happiness, and Beth returned the kiss with the same depth of feeling.

"You're sure we have to wait until Gillian and the twins leave to get married?" he asked huskily.

Beth had been helping Gillian sort and pack, but Gillian kept changing her mind about this and that, so much so that Beth sometimes wondered if the reconciliation was ever actually going to take place. "If she isn't gone in two weeks, we'll get married anyway," Beth guaranteed recklessly.

Guy grinned. "I'm going to hold you to that."

He produced a wicker basket from the car and gaily led the way to the dining room for a celebration picnic. There he stopped short.

"I forgot, no chairs," he said in dismay.

"No problem," Beth assured him. She grabbed a napkin from the basket and polished away the dust on the table. "Some people may eat *at* their table; we'll eat *on* ours."

So saying, she unceremoniously hopped up on the enormous table, plopped down cross-legged in her full-skirted dress, waited for him to offer the blessing, and then calmly started serving the sandwiches and lemonade as if she were the hostess at some elegant and very proper meal. Guy looked nonplused for a moment, then joined her on the table, swinging Joey up to a safe spot between his outspread legs.

"Madam has a very creative imagination," he said politely.

"Madam is starved," she said, and chomped into a sandwich.

They ate and talked and made plans. And in between plans and sandwiches there were kisses and laughter, good-natured teasings, and even a small but heated argument about whether the bed in the bedroom should remain where it was or be moved to the opposite wall.

"Very well, you win," Guy finally grumbled. "The bed gets moved. But just for that I get first choice on which side I want to sleep on." His tone challenged but his eyes glinted with tease.

The vision of the two of them sharing that big bed was enough to pinken Beth's cheeks again, although inwardly she suspected the blush was as much anticipation as embarrassment. She did love him so very much! But all she said was a demure, "That sounds fair." And then went on talking about painting the interior walls a light cream color, as if they'd merely been discussing colors and walls all along.

"The first thing to do is bring in electricity," Guy said.

"Put a modern stove and refrigerator in the kitchen."

"Install another bathroom. Put in new kitchen cupboards." Guy grinned. "Fill the nursery with babies."

"An even dozen would be nice, I think," Beth said thoughtfully.

Guy visibly gulped at the number. "Babies?"

Beth poked him in the stomach with a finger and flashed him her own teasing grin. "No, silly. Kitchen cupboards."

Guy tossed the remnants of his sandwich in the basket. He put his arms around Beth, careful not to disturb Joey, who had quietly drifted off to sleep after his lunch.

"I love you, Beth, so very much. I love you when you're serious and I love you when you're silly. I love you because you're courageous and loyal and good-hearted. I love you for so many reasons it would take a lifetime to list them all! And that's how long I intend to take telling you all the reasons I love you." His teasing tones had gone tender and serious. "The only thing I regret is that we had to lose Sylvia and Mark in order to find each other."

Beth swallowed and nodded. She leaned her forehead against his, and they were both silent for a long, thoughtful moment. The Lord's ways in such matters were not easily understood.

"But we'll bring up their son as they would have wanted him to be brought up," she vowed.

They stayed at the house until dusk, loath to leave this spot they had chosen as home. The moon rose to silhouette a lone saguaro on the crest of a nearby hill, timeless and serene, the perfect ending to what Beth knew she would always remember as a perfect day.

Eighteen

G ardiner residence."

Beth answered the telephone in the midst of individually wrapping Gillian's numerous bottles of perfume and lotions. Gillian had taken the twins to a movie matinee. Mr. Gardiner was in California on business, Millie had the afternoon off, and Joey was napping on the screened-in back porch.

"May I speak with Annie Thompson, please?" The voice was unfamiliar, male, formal.

Beth's nerves skittered in a way they hadn't for some time, and her first panicky thought was: *Nat Wilkerson has found us!*

A reassuring thought—that she was no longer alone in a battle with Nat Wilkerson; Guy was with her now—allowed the jolt to recede until she could swallow and say, "This is Mrs. Thompson." But the man's next words were on such a different subject that it took her a moment to shift gears.

"Mrs. Thompson, my name is Arthur Rafferty. I'm an art dealer from San Francisco, and I'm opening a gallery here in Phoenix. I've been inquiring about local artists whose work is of the caliber I want to offer in the gallery, and your name has come up several times."

"It has?" Beth felt foolish even as she said the surprised words. Hardly the proper reaction for a professional, high-caliber artist!

"I was wondering if I might inspect some of your current work while I'm in town?"

What Beth wanted to do was gleefully jump for joy at this unexpected opportunity, but she managed to say with what she hoped was professional calm, "I do commissioned paintings primarily, but I might be interested in placing a few things with a gallery."

"Would this afternoon be convenient? I could come by your studio."

Her "studio," a corner of her bedroom in cooler weather, the backyard in these hot months! She didn't elaborate on that, however, and simply said, "I'd be pleased to show you what I have on hand."

She gave him the address and then spread everything she had available around the living room, where he could also see the framed painting of the twins that was so often admired. She angled the portrait of the ranch cowboy in his boots and chaps against the back of an upholstered chair, below it placing the one of Joey in the cowboy's lap. Landscapes weren't her strong point, but she had a rustic barn scene that she'd also done at the ranch. She hurriedly unpacked the portrait of Gillian to add to the showing. In addition, she had an unfinished, commissioned painting of a brother and sister, and a series of sketches of Joey.

Hardly a large or impressive showing, she fretted. But the doorbell was already ringing.

The man removed his hat when she opened the door. "I'm Arthur Rafferty, and I'm here to see Annie Thompson," he said politely.

He was fiftyish, but his tall figure bore no trace of middle-aged stoutness. He had a distinguished gleam of silver at his temples and a neat mustache, and even in this heat he wore a suave dark suit. In the living room he moved slowly from painting to painting, his expression unrevealing except for a small grimace when he studied the portrait of the twins. Beth's high hopes plunged until he murmured, "Some people seem to feel that if one gilt curlicue is good, a dozen are better," and she realized that it was the fussy frame he disdained, an opinion she shared with him.

Finally he turned and looked at her. "I must say, Mrs. Thompson, that I'm surprised."

"Surprised?" she repeated warily.

"Surprised and impressed. I'd heard you were very talented, but I also knew you'd done mostly portraits of children." He smiled. "And parents are not the most discerning of art critics when it comes to seeing their small darlings preserved on canvas for posterity."

Beth didn't know whether she was being complimented or criticized, and merely smiled politely.

"But these paintings show an impressive talent." He leaned forward with hands clasped behind his back to study the painting of the cowboy and Joey. "What you've done with the contrast of leathery cowboy and childish innocence is quite remarkable. Is it for sale?"

"Why, yes, I suppose it is."

"And the others?"

"The unfinished portrait is commissioned, and the one of the woman is taken." She decided honesty was best. "I haven't much available, because I'm really more governess than professional artist."

He glanced around. "And a maid and housekeeper as well?"

200

"There's also a woman who cooks and keeps up the house, but she has the afternoon off."

"Well, Mrs. Thompson, commendable as such employment may be, as a connoisseur of art, I hate to see someone of your talent wasting her time on it." He smiled. "However, once the gallery opens I think you'll find a new world opening up for you." He picked up one of the rough sketches of Joey. "This is one of your young charges?"

"No, that's my own son." Calling Joey her own son came naturally now. "That's also him in the painting with the cowboy, of course."

Mr. Rafferty outlined his plans for the gallery. Even in these hard times Phoenix was growing in popularity as a winter resort for wealthy tourists, and he planned to capitalize on that.

"And you really do want my paintings for your gallery?"

"Yes indeed. Although...would it hurt your feelings if I suggest you stick with portraits, especially of children, rather than landscapes?" He arched an elegant eyebrow.

Beth laughed. She knew her limitations in the area of landscapes. "No, you won't hurt my feelings, Mr. Rafferty."

"Good. I'll be in touch, then, as my plans for the gallery progress. But in the meantime..." He pulled out his wallet and eyed the painting of Joey and the cowboy again. "I'm prepared to offer you a hundred and fifty dollars as an outright purchase for this one."

The amount was several times her salary. "Why?" she gasped.

Mr. Rafferty laughed. "The first thing to learn as an up-and-coming young artist, Mrs. Thompson, is never to look astonished that someone is willing to pay a good price for your work. Actually, I have a customer in San Francisco in mind. I could ask for the painting on consignment, but, since you don't know me from some itinerant snake-oil salesman, who might or might not send on your share of the sale, I thought you might prefer cash in hand."

"Cash would be nice," Beth admitted.

He handed over the money, then dabbed lightly at his perspiring brow with a handkerchief. "After the cooler climate of San Francisco I find the intensity of the heat here a bit intimidating," he apologized.

"Would you like something to drink? You do look warm."

He nodded, and she got a glass of lemonade from the kitchen. At the same time Joey woke from his nap and started a demanding cry of "Mama, mama, mama!" Beth brought him back to the living room with her. He was bare except for a diaper, his sweet little body warm and damp.

"And this is our fine young model for the sketches and painting?"

"Yes. This is my son, Joey." Joey was usually friendly with everyone but turned his head away when Mr. Rafferty held out his arms. "I guess he's not quite awake yet."

"He looks about the age of our youngest grandson."

"Will you be living here in Phoenix after you open the art gallery?" she added as he sipped the lemonade.

"No. I'll be coming here frequently, but I doubt we'd ever leave San Francisco. Our three children are grown and live nearby." He smiled. "And I'm sure you know how grandparents are about their grandchildren."

Yes, Beth remembered that wonderful attachment from her childhood. Unfortunately, it was not a relationship Joey would ever know. She smiled and nodded anyway.

"The Lord is everywhere, of course, but we also wouldn't want to leave our church in San Francisco. Madeline is very active in the missionary society." Mr. Rafferty carefully set the glass on a coaster and picked up his newly purchased painting. "I'm going to make money on this," he warned cheerfully.

"I hope you do."

Guy had barely gotten home from the newspaper when Beth dashed over with an excited story about a Mr. Rafferty from San Francisco who was opening an art gallery in Phoenix and wanted to exhibit and sell her paintings. "And look at this!"

She fanned twenties and tens on his kitchen table like a winning hand of cards, then exuberantly flung her arms around him. "He bought one of my paintings! We can buy chairs to go around our dining room table! Paint for the walls…"

"Mat—" He'd started to say "mattress for the bed" but thought better of it and just grinned and kissed her instead, although her rising color suggested she knew exactly what he'd started to say. He was not very good at hiding his eagerness to become a bridegroom, he had to admit. He kissed her again. "I'm delighted for you, sweetheart. But not surprised. Because you're good, very good."

They celebrated by splurging a little of the money on eating dinner out. "I've never treated *you!*" Beth exclaimed. Guy was glad to see her so happy.

Yet after he'd taken her home and was lying on his cot in the backyard looking up at the stars, he couldn't rid himself of a certain clinging uneasiness. Why?

Could he be one of those selfish, narrow-minded men who deep down envied or resented a woman's success?

He knocked that ugly ball around in his mind for a while and concluded he was not guilty of that. He wanted Beth to have the recognition her talent deserved.

Did he suspect that this man was out to take unscrupulous

advantage of Beth's artistic talent in some way? Given the fact that Rafferty had been forthright in saying he intended to make money on the painting he purchased from her, that seemed unlikely. He also hadn't asked for any money from Beth, with some wild claim that an investment would guarantee success. So at this point it would be unfair to accuse the man of being some confidence-game operator.

Was he suspicious because he doubted Beth had as much talent as Rafferty indicated, which might suggest he was something other than the art dealer he claimed to be?

No. Beth had talent, plenty of it. She also deserved a break, a chance to show everyone how good she was, and this might well be that important big opportunity.

But it wouldn't hurt, he decided, to do a little checking on Mr. Arthur Rafferty, self-proclaimed art dealer and gallery owner of San Francisco.

In the next few days, everything fell neatly into place.

Mr. Rafferty called to tell Beth he'd found the perfect location for the gallery and was negotiating a lease. Guy signed papers to start their purchase of the house. Gillian picked a departure date and shipped several trunks. Beth and Guy made arrangements with Pastor Merriman to officiate at a small wedding ceremony. Often Beth just stopped whatever she was doing to close her eyes and, giddy with love and joy, give thanks to the Lord.

Mr. Rafferty called again to say his client in San Francisco was also interested in the painting of the cowboy alone. When he came for it they sat in the backyard drinking iced tea and talking about everything from art to families and Christian faith. Beth was eager for Guy to meet him, and suggested it for that evening, but Arthur regretfully said he had another artist's work to inspect.

He stood to go. "Annie—" They'd reached a comfortable first-names rapport by now. "I hope you won't think me impertinent, but you tell me you're a governess, yet I never see you 'governessing'?"

Beth smiled and explained that Gillian usually took the twins swimming at her friend's pool on these torrid days. "Actually, my position here will end soon. Gillian and the twins are moving east."

"And what will you be doing then?"

Beth didn't try to hide her pride and happiness. Sometimes she just wanted to stand in the street and shout to the world how much she loved Guy! "I'm getting married in a few days."

"Why, how wonderful, my dear! I'm very happy for you."

An exciting new thought occurred to her. "In fact, we'll be coming to San Francisco on our honeymoon. Perhaps we can visit your gallery!"

"Yes, that would be lovely. I'll look forward to it."

As it turned out, Guy wouldn't have had time to meet Mr. Rafferty that evening anyway. He phoned to say that the editor had abruptly quit, so he was taking over the newspaper sooner than he had anticipated. He sounded harried but exhilarated.

"The only thing is, this doesn't fit our honeymoon plans."

"We can honeymoon right here. Just as long as we're together—"

"You can bet I'm not about to let you honeymoon with anyone else!"

Beth told him about her latest meeting with Arthur. Guy was silent for a moment, the only sound on the line the ring of another telephone and the background clatter of a typewriter.

"Beth, has Rafferty ever told you where in San Francisco his gallery is located? What the name of it is?"

"No, but if you're interested I can ask him."

"Yes, do that. And…be careful, okay? We really don't know anything about this man, and now he's hanging around the house, drinking your tea."

"Guy Wilkerson, are you jealous?" she teased. "I know I said he was handsome and elegant and suave…"

Guy laughed lightly. "Isn't that enough to make any man jealous?"

"Perhaps I should have added that he's middle-aged, has a wife, three grown children, and a handful of grandchildren he's crazy about. They're very active in their church, and he grows roses."

"Okay, sounds as if he has solid gold credentials. Just…be careful anyway, okay?"

Nineteen

Arthur called again the following morning with an invitation for Beth to come downtown and meet the contractor he'd engaged to remodel the gallery building. "I think the views of an artist will be most helpful. We'll all have lunch and then inspect the building together."

The invitation both surprised and flattered Beth. Gillian had already said she was taking the twins swimming again, so that would be no problem. "I'll have to bring Joey, of course."

"That would be a bit awkward for a business meeting… Perhaps the housekeeper could take care of him for a couple of hours?"

"Hold on a moment, and I'll check with Millie."

Millie said she'd watch Joey, and Beth returned with that information. Arthur named a downtown restaurant and they agreed to meet at one o'clock.

But while Beth was slipping into a dress and shoes suitable for tromping around an empty building, Millie rushed upstairs with unfortunate news. Her cousin had just taken a tumble, and Millie had to take her to the doctor. Beth assured her this was no problem; she doubted Arthur would really object even though he'd discouraged her from bringing Joey.

Arthur did, however, look quite distressed when the waitress led Beth to his table in the restaurant. "I thought you were leaving him with the housekeeper!"

Beth briefly explained why she'd brought Joey. "But if having him here is a problem, I won't stay."

"No, no, it's fine." He waved her to a chair and picked up a menu. "What would you like to eat?"

"Shouldn't we wait until the other guest arrives to order?"

He blinked, almost as if he'd forgotten the contractor was coming. "Yes, I suppose so." He closed the menu.

Then he fidgeted. He glanced out the window. Took a sip of water. Straightened his silverware. Sipped more water.

"Is something wrong, Arthur?"

"Oh, no. Just a poor night's sleep. How did you get here?"

"I splurged on a taxi." She smiled. "Getting accustomed to being a rich and famous artist."

Arthur did not respond to her small attempt to poke fun at her prospects of fame and fortune. "Does Guy know you're here?" he asked.

"No. He's so busy at the newspaper now that I don't like to call."

Arthur fidgeted with his silverware again. He looked at his pocket watch. The contractor was a little late, but neither that nor Joey's presence seemed enough to warrant his jittery agitation.

"Arthur, something seems wrong. You are so distracted."

He looked at Joey. "Maybe it's just that I've been away from Marcella and the grandchildren for too long, and I miss them so much. Could I hold him, Annie?"

He sounded so woebegone that even though Joey had never made up to him as he did with most people, she set him in

Arthur's lap. Joey squirmed and scrunched his face as if he might cry, but Arthur played a game of peekaboo with his napkin that soon had Joey giggling. Arthur checked his pocket watch again.

"I'm wondering if the contractor didn't misunderstand and go directly to the building. Do you suppose you could run over there and check? My arthritic leg just isn't up to walking that far."

"How far is it?"

"Just go around the corner, down five blocks and over two. It's a brick building. His name is Martin Wheeler."

The idea of walking that far carrying Joey in the heat was not appealing, but Beth reached across the table for him.

"That's too far to carry a big guy like this. I can take care of him for a few minutes. That's what grandpas are for, right?" he asked Joey with a jiggle and bounce of his knee.

Beth hesitated, but the walk would definitely be easier without Joey. He was now engrossed in exploring Arthur's mustache. "I'll be back in a few minutes, then."

Outside, the midday air hit her like a hot wall. She turned the corner, *five blocks this direction....*

An odd thought struck her. She didn't recall telling Arthur Guy's name. She'd told him she was getting married, but she was certain she hadn't mentioned a name. And why was he so uncharacteristically nervous and distracted?

Be careful, Guy had said.

She'd immediately jumped to the playful conclusion that Guy was exhibiting a twinge of male jealousy, but had he some deeper concern?

Another disturbing jolt. *Marcella.* Arthur had called his wife Marcella today, but hadn't he referred to her as Madeline before?

Something was peculiar here. Maybe more than peculiar.

Beth suddenly saw the situation with ominous clarity.

After months of being so careful, looking over her shoulder and watching every step, now she had blithely walked off and left Joey alone with a near-stranger.

She was already running even as the thought blazed across her mind, her heart pounding faster than her feet as fear clogged her throat. She raced to the corner, skidding around it.

And there was Arthur, shoving a howling Joey into his car.

Guy dropped into the chair behind his cluttered desk with a silent groan. Had every bolt and screw in the *Courier* been primed to collapse the minute he took over? Just since yesterday the delivery truck had broken down, top reporter Scotch Wilson had defected to the rival newspaper, and the machinery that was supposed to fold the printed sheets had started ripping them to shreds instead.

What he needed was the cheerful, soothing sound of Beth's voice.

He'd tried to call her half an hour ago but had gotten no answer. He tried again now—no response. He felt a ripple of alarm. Odd.

No. Frustrating, perhaps, but not *odd*. She could be running an errand or painting in the backyard. She might have tried to call him while he was away from his desk.

His fingers tattooed the desktop. In spite of those plausible rationalizations, he was not reassured. He had not, in fact, been able to shake a niggling apprehension ever since Arthur Rafferty's arrival. He was still waiting for more information in response to his telephone and telegraph inquiries to San Francisco.

So far there was nothing to prove Rafferty wasn't who and

what he said he was. There was also nothing to prove he *was* a bona fide art dealer and gallery owner in San Francisco.

And wasn't that in itself cause for alarm? Shouldn't a reputable businessman be more visible, more well known, in his home area than Rafferty appeared to be? He reached an abrupt decision. Even at the risk of annoying Beth, he was going to demand that Rafferty provide positive proof of his identity and authenticity. In fact, maybe he ought to run out to the house right now.

A young man's head appeared in the open doorway. "Mr. Wilkerson, something's gone wrong with the Linotype machine. It's all gummed up."

Guy groaned again. He'd wanted a newspaper...and now he had one!

Beth's headlong charge flung Arthur into the fender. She grabbed at the door handle, but he jerked upright and caught her wrist. She twisted and struggled, panting in the heat.

"Let me go! I want my baby!"

"Annie, please! What's wrong? People are staring!" Arthur's always perfectly knotted tie now hung askew, and a button on his suit dangled by a thread from her reckless assault.

"You're stealing my baby!"

"Stealing your baby?" he echoed. He looked around, as if appealing to some passerby to explain this woman who had mysteriously turned wild and hysterical.

Beth stopped struggling, suddenly less certain of her accusations. Joey had quit shrieking and now grinned at her with his little nose and fingers pressed against the window. She felt a bit as she did when she nabbed the wrong twin for some misdemeanor, but she wasn't yet ready to back down. "If you're not stealing him, what *are* you doing?"

"When you got out of sight, Joey started crying. I realized I'd been thoughtless asking you to walk all that way in this heat. I decided to follow and pick you up in the car." He patted her shoulder awkwardly. "Look, Annie, why don't I just take you and Joey on home? We'll arrange this meeting for some other time."

She peered at him more closely. Poor Arthur. Such a proper, dignified gentleman, and here she was screeching accusations and making a spectacle out of his innocent attempt to be considerate.

"I'm sorry. Perhaps the heat. I really would like to go on home, if you don't mind."

He opened the car door and she slid inside, hugging Joey close on her lap in spite of the heat. Even though there hadn't been any real danger, her heart still thudded like a pulsing fist in her chest.

She leaned her head against the seat, eyes closed, feeling oddly drained, and the car turned several corners before going soothingly straight. When she opened her eyes a few minutes later, she didn't recognize the street or tourist cabins. "This isn't the way home!"

"I have an errand to run out this way. I didn't think you'd mind."

Another few miles, and the scattered businesses and fields gave way to desert. The reddish cliffs of the Superstitions loomed in the distance, and now Beth knew where they were. This was the way they'd come the day of the picnic. What errand could Arthur possibly have out here? An apprehension suddenly constricted her throat like a shrinking rope. She looked over at him, so suave yet grandfatherly. Surely she was wrong! Yet she was not at all comfortable with this odd excursion.

"Arthur, would you turn around, please? I want to go home. You can take care of your errand some other time."

Arthur sighed as if he regretted what he had to say. "I am sorry, my dear. This isn't the way things were supposed to go at all."

"What do you mean?" She asked the question even as the specter of truth rose like some monster out of the dark to confront her.

"You were supposed to leave Joey at home. A...what should I call him? Acquaintance? Certainly I wouldn't call such an uncouth ruffian a friend, and accomplice has such an unsavory ring."

"You're not an art dealer. You're a...kidnapper!"

"This acquaintance was supposed to remove Joey from the house while I kept you busy. A bit sooner than was originally planned, but we had to hurry things along when you spoke of visiting my 'gallery' in San Francisco. A ring of the doorbell and a mysterious package were to keep the housekeeper occupied while he went in the back way and got Joey. Then he was to deliver the child to me. All very smooth and neat. I even brought supplies for the baby."

He tilted his head toward the rear seat, where Beth saw a dark satchel with bulging sides.

"There's canned milk, crackers, fresh water, canned fruit and vegetables, diapers, baby bottles, everything a baby needs." He spoke as if proud of his foresight, his earlier nervousness gone. "But now it appears the three of us will be traveling together. I do hope there won't be any difficulties or awkward complications."

Did he think she was simply going to sit here demurely and let this happen? The first time the car slowed, she'd just grab Joey and run.

He reached into a pocket and withdrew a small but deadly looking gun. He set it within easy reach on the floorboard near his right foot. "It is loaded," he added pleasantly.

Beth momentarily found herself too stunned to say anything. She leaned her head back against the seat and offered a jumbled prayer for strength and courage and help.

"But I do object to being called a *kidnapper.* I understand that this…ah, transfer, is simply to return the child to his proper guardian. A very rich grandfather, I believe."

"Is that how you justify what you're doing?"

He smiled. "Actually, the money I'm being paid effectively oils any small squeaks of conscience that might trouble me. Look, Annie…" He paused. "But that isn't your real name either, is it?"

"I'm sure you know exactly who I am."

"Yes. Well, I want to assure you that you're in no real danger. I may skirt the finer points of the law occasionally, but I'm not a murderer of women and children."

"The gun is just for decoration?" she snapped, suddenly angry at herself. How could she have been so blind and foolish? She saw so clearly now how he had wormed his way into her confidence and shrewdly learned the household schedule. How he had managed to convince her of his innocence even as he was stealing Joey!

"I hope that is exactly what the gun is—a decoration. Although I'd advise you not to try anything rash, such as grabbing Joey and making a run for it," he added as if he'd read her mind. "It would have been so much more convenient if you'd simply carried out the errand I sent you on. Why did you rush back?"

There was a wild, disorienting unreality to this calm discussion. But nothing unreal about that deadly little gun at his feet.

Could she get hold of it? She tried not to let a drift of her gaze give that thought away. "It occurred to me that there were inconsistencies in things you'd said."

"Inconsistencies?"

"First your wife was Madeline. Then she was Marcella."

He smiled ruefully. "It can be so difficult to remember the name of a nonexistent wife."

A nonexistent wife. Beth had already figured out that there was no art gallery, but... "It was all a lie? The children and grandchildren, the church in San Francisco?"

"I'm afraid so."

She swallowed. Odd, how disappointed she felt that none of it had been true. "Who are you, really?"

"Ummmm." He paused, considering the question. "I don't think I should tell you that, Annie—no, Bethany, isn't it? Because I do intend to let you go when this is over, and I wouldn't want you to run to the authorities with some incriminating information."

Beth was not reassured. If everything Arthur Rafferty...or whoever he was...had told her was a glib lie, why not this, too? Perhaps the real plan now, given these changed circumstances, was a lonely grave for her somewhere out here in the desert.

Beth stared at the harsh, heat-baked landscape of rock and cactus and scraggly creosote bush, and tried not to see herself lying out there. They'd swung south of the Superstitions now, and the mountains rose stark and savage under a shadow of rapidly massing thunderclouds. There were few cars on the road. Even if she managed to get herself and Joey out of the car, she'd never be able to flag down help before Arthur recaptured her. Or shot her down. And they'd never survive if she tried to flee into the desert with Joey.

"Guy will come after us, you know," she said suddenly. "He

won't let you get away with abducting us like this."

Beth was bluffing, but Arthur glanced at her sharply.

"He has no idea where we are," Arthur scoffed after giving her claim a brief consideration. "No idea what kind of car we're in, or anything else to guide or help him."

Guy had God! But what she said was another bluff. "He knows both your car and license number. I was taken in by you, but he was already suspicious. The housekeeper will tell him where I was meeting you. He'll have no problem figuring out what route we're taking. He's probably chasing us down right now!"

Everything, except the fact that Guy was suspicious of Arthur, was raw fiction, but Arthur abruptly swore with a flare of anger that made her flinch. "I was warned he could be dangerous. And big trouble." His gaze darted to the rearview mirror.

Beth also looked back, hopeful in spite of knowing Guy couldn't possibly be racing to catch them. The road was empty as far back as she could see, the only movement the dancing shimmers of heat. She had never felt more alone. Yet she wasn't alone, she reminded herself fiercely. God was with her!

When she looked ahead again, she saw the only indication in miles that humans actually lived out here, a sign with a faded painting of a prospector and the words GAS - EATS - GRO-CERIES 2 Mi.

Arthur glanced down at the gas gauge. "I don't know how far it is to the next gas, so we're going to fill up here. Don't try anything."

Not try anything? Beth clamped the fingernails of one hand into the palm of the other to steady the tremble of both hands, the grip so savage she felt a crunch of bone. This might be the *only* chance she'd have to do something.

Her muscles tensed. Flight or fight. Whatever it took.

Twenty

Guy stretched his shoulders against the leather seat, tired but victorious. In spite of everything that had gone wrong, the *Courier* was on the streets. An hour late…but with a front-page piece about some behind-the-scenes activities of the city council that was going to make Phoenix rattle and shake.

He glanced down the street as he slid out of the car. He wanted to talk to Beth about Rafferty right away.

A police car was just pulling away from the Gardiner house. Guy slammed the car door and lit out on a run, his earlier uneasiness clumping into a ragged knot of fear. He hammered on the front door.

A harried-looking Millie opened it. "Oh, I'm so glad to see you!"

The twins raced down the hallway and threw themselves on him. "We got robbed!" Adrian sounded both gleeful and scared.

"He got my pearl earrings!" Gillian yelled from upstairs.

"What happened?" Guy asked Millie.

"Sometime this afternoon, while no one was home, someone broke in the back door and…"

Gillian appeared at the head of the stairs, face flushed with heat and frustration. "I should have gone back to Boston weeks ago! And where *is* Annie? She's never here when I want her anymore."

Guy grabbed Millie by the shoulders. "How long has she been gone?"

"I'm not sure." Millie rattled through some long, involved story about taking her cousin to the doctor. "So I couldn't watch Joey after all, and Annie said she'd just take him along."

Gillian yelled something about a missing bracelet. The twins wrapped themselves around his legs, talking at breakneck speed and bullhorn loudness. The telephone shrilled. But in the midst of all this pandemonium only one thing mattered to Guy. "Along *where?*"

"Why, to meet that art man. But she should have been home by now."

Hours before now, Guy thought bleakly. He slammed more questions at her, but Millie knew only that Annie was to meet Mr. Rafferty somewhere at one o'clock. He questioned Gillian too, but she was no help, more annoyed than concerned about Annie's absence.

Millie *was* concerned about Beth. "It just isn't like her. If she tried to stop someone from breaking in…"

Millie's frightened gaze targeted a smudge on the wall. For a moment Guy thought it was blood, but when he knelt and looked closer he saw that it was just a smear of dirt at twins'-fingertip height.

The mundane discovery did not reassure him. It was possible Beth's meeting with Rafferty was simply running overlong, he conceded. A far worse possibility was that she'd interrupted a burglary, and the thief had panicked and forced her to accompany him. But Guy doubted that. No blood. No signs of scuffle. And it didn't make sense that a common burglar would make off with a woman and baby. And then there was Rafferty, suave, slick, art-buying Rafferty. Coincidence?

No. The whole thing reeked of Nat Wilkerson.

But Nat only wanted Joey. Why was Beth also missing?

Because what Nat wanted, Nat got, Guy thought bitterly. And it wouldn't matter to him what happened to one innocent woman who got in the way. *Lord, now what?* he asked as he clenched his fists in anger and fear. *Show me what to do!*

The police. He wheeled and slammed the door behind him, cutting off Gillian's complaints without so much as a backward glance.

Arthur stopped the car by the faded pump, where an inch of yellow-orange gasoline showed in the glass. The place looked deserted, only a crumpled candy wrapper and a fresh oil stain on the ground suggesting it was still in business, until a tan hound ambled out and sniffed their tires.

Okay, this was it. Beth tightened one arm around Joey and surreptitiously inched her other hand toward the door handle. She'd make a run for the little store. Arthur wouldn't dare shoot her down in front of witnesses.

The screen door opened, a shadowy figure behind it. Arthur grabbed at Joey, Beth hung on. For a few silent moments they wrestled over the baby, but when Joey let out a howl of pain, Beth let go.

An old man limped toward the pump, cane in one hand. "Help yuh?"

"Fill her up, please."

The old man cocked a hand around one ear. "Eh?"

Arthur repeated his request, louder, and Beth's hopes plummeted.

The old man industriously worked the handle of the gas

pump back and forth, and gas surged upward within the glass. He and Arthur small-talked about the looming thunderstorm, the old man's voice overly loud, as if Arthur, not he, were the deaf one. Joey fussed, wanting to get back to Beth, but Arthur bounced him in his lap and loudly said something about his "getting used to your ol' grandpa."

A new idea pulsed into Beth's mind. "I think I'll go inside and get a soda pop," she interrupted casually.

"I'll be in soon's I get through here," the old man said. "Only me here now, since my wife passed on last year."

"Would you happen to have a telephone?" Arthur asked.

"Nope. Might get 'lectricity later this year, though."

Arthur looked at Beth and smiled. "Still want a soda pop?"

Beth slumped against the seat. Without a phone, he knew she couldn't surreptitiously try to summon Guy or the police. Arthur smiled again and silently proclaimed his victory by handing Joey back to her.

But there was another way....

Beth waited until paying for the gasoline momentarily diverted Arthur's attention. She leaned over, pretending to tie her shoelace, then snaked her left hand toward the gun.

Arthur didn't even look at her, but his heel stomped down on her knuckles. She yelped in pain and yanked her crushed hand back. The old man peered in the window. Even he had heard that anguished cry.

"Somethin' wrong?"

"I think my daughter accidentally twisted her sprained wrist again," Arthur said smoothly.

Beth marveled at how glibly he again explained away an incriminating situation. She pressed the injured hand against her leg, pain radiating from fingernails to shoulder, tears sharp in her eyes.

Flight or fight? Beth slumped back in the seat. She'd tried both. And they were still trapped.

Arthur gave the old man an amiable wave as the car pulled away from the pump. Beth hugged Joey close, burying her face in the curve of his damp little neck, desperately trying not to give in to pain and despair. A few hundred yards farther on, Arthur abruptly whipped the car off the main road and onto another narrow, rocky road leading off to the left. Beth rammed out her good hand to keep from crashing into the windshield.

"What are you doing?" she gasped.

Arthur wheeled the car behind a jumble of boulders and turned off the engine. "A car was coming up on us. Fast. As if it were after someone. The old man at the station may tell him we were just there."

Arthur thought it could be Guy! And he was plainly rattled by the possibility. Beth knew it couldn't be Guy, and yet she felt a wild budding of hope. Maybe, by some miracle, he *would* come!

They sat there in strained silence, Arthur craning to watch behind them even though the jumbled rocks blocked view of the main road. After several minutes he grabbed a map from the side pocket of the door and studied it.

"Where are we going?" Beth asked nervously when he started the engine and, instead of returning to the main road, continued on the same rough side road.

"We'll cut across here to a road heading north. Your boyfriend won't be looking for us out here."

No, Guy would never look for them here, Beth agreed, her hopes falling like a barometer in a storm. Neither were they apt to run into anyone else, she thought as the narrow road wound ever farther into the harsh, barren mountains. Only the road itself gave evidence that other humans had ever been here; all else was rock and cactus and bare, gritty dirt with the occasional glitter of some minute speck of mineral. Running water had at some time eroded the tracks of the old road into rough gullies. Rocks, washed in or fallen from above or exposed by the weather, littered the road, some so large that the car jerked and bucked to surmount them. Sometimes one side of the road dropped away to a canyon, and she dared not lean to peer out the window to see the bottom because it felt as if the very shift of her weight might plunge the car over the edge. Her hand ached, the knuckles so stiff she could barely flex her fingers.

She tried not to think what a perfect place this was to dump a body, afraid the very thought might ooze into Arthur's consciousness. Thunderclouds blotted out the sun now, and thunder rumbled around them. It vibrated the earth, the car, and Beth herself, as if it were inside her. Joey whimpered fearfully. The engine growled and strained on the upgrades; the brakes squeaked on the downgrades. The air, electrified by the storm, raised the fine hairs on Beth's arms.

A few huge raindrops hit the dusty hood, the splotches large as saucers. To their left an old mine tunnel yawned like an open mouth, the wooden tooth of a broken timber dangling from the top. Another dark hole penetrated the hillside several hundred yards ahead of them. Perhaps the mines were why the road had once been built, Beth guessed. And, along with the old holes in the earth, long ago abandoned.

"Arthur, this road isn't going anywhere!" Beth finally cried. "Can't you see that? How far have we come? Five miles? Ten? It can't be the connecting road you saw on the map!"

"Maybe not," he conceded in a frustrated growl. A few hundred feet farther on, he stopped the car. "Okay, we'll turn around here."

"There isn't enough room!"

Arthur angled the front of the car into the steep hillside. He backed a few inches, pulled ahead, backed again. Behind them, the hill dropped off into a boulder-strewn ravine. Sweat poured off his face as he repeated the maneuver several times. More raindrops splatted hood and windshield. Impatiently, he tried to make the next back-and-forth maneuver the final one.

"Don't!" Beth screamed. "You're going too far!"

With infinite slowness the rear of the car settled downward. The hood tilted upward. Beth leaned forward, willing it not to go. "No!"

Inexorably, gathering drunken speed, it went, crashing, sliding, tilting. Beth simply wrapped herself around Joey, blindly protecting him as best she could. Something crashed into her shoulder. A scream...hers! A weird rotation of sky and rock. Shattering glass, Joey's shrieks.

When the car finally came to a halt, all Beth could do was clutch Joey and whisper a prayer of thanks that they were still alive. "It's okay, sweetie," she soothed as she tried to collect her senses in the disorienting jumble. "We're okay."

Were they? Beth hastily took inventory. Joey was still howling, but the howl had a healthy strength. She found scratches on herself, but nothing more. Arthur? In astonishment she realized he'd been flung into the rear seat. The satchel was wedged against the steering wheel. Arthur groaned and moved. The car shivered, and only then did Beth realize they weren't yet at the bottom of the ravine, that the car was precariously perched against a boulder. Rain pelted the car now, as if gathering fury for a full onslaught, but they dare not stay inside.

She nudged Joey toward the door on the upper side, carefully sliding after him. She pushed Joey out the window and crawled out behind him. She scrabbled and clawed up the steep incline. At the top, rain-battered and panting, she heard a hoarse cry from below.

"Annie! Annie!"

She peered over the edge. Through the savage blur of rain she saw Arthur struggling up the ravine behind her, arthritic leg dragging like a bent branch. Reluctantly, dredging up every ounce of Christian generosity she possessed, she knelt and stretched out a hand to him.

"That old mine shaft!" he gasped. "We can take shelter there!"

Beth agreed, then halted. After the storm was over it would still take hours to hike out to civilization; Joey had to have food and water before then.

She thrust Joey into Arthur's arms. At the moment, Arthur was probably the least of the dangers threatening Joey. And they were on more equal terms now. He had no gun. "You carry him to the tunnel."

She edged down the steep ravine to the car, clutching at bits of rock and grass to keep from tumbling headlong. At the car she reached through the window and snatched the satchel, then fought her way up to the road again.

She could barely make out Arthur's hunched, hobbling figure ahead of her in the pounding deluge. She struggled after him, the heavy satchel banging her thighs and knees. Her wet hair fell in her eyes; her dress clung to her skin; she ached everywhere. Wind joined the rain; a shrieking gust shoved her like the thrust of a malicious fist.

Yet in spite of rain and wind she hesitated at the yawning mouth of the mine tunnel. She couldn't go in there! She forced down the sudden jolt of claustrophobia and ducked under the snaggletooth of broken timber.

Inside, a jumble of more fallen timbers angled against the

crumbling walls. She edged farther into the tunnel, back to where Arthur and Joey were huddled out of reach of the wind-blown rain. She resolutely set a time limit: no more than fifteen minutes in here. After that, no matter if raindrops the size of baseballs were falling and winds gusting at typhoon force, she was getting out and taking Joey with her. Already the walls felt as if they were closing in. She set the satchel down and retrieved Joey, using her body to warm and comfort him.

"Here," Arthur said, "I'll fix you something to sit on." He stepped around her and yanked on an angled timber.

And the world collapsed around them.

CHAPTER

Twenty-One

❧

Roar of falling earth. Rain of rock and dirt. Blinding, choking, smothering dust. And on and on went the earth-rending
rumble that reduced ordinary thunder to no more than the
pretentious shaking of a sky-bound fist.

Panic and terror swallowed Beth like a devouring monster.
She couldn't think, couldn't breathe, couldn't move. All she
could do was cover Joey with her body and offer a prayer so
intense that it was beyond words.

Yet eventually the rumble did die away, until the only
sounds were Beth's own ragged breathing and the small hiss of
earth still trickling through some unseen crevice. Even Joey was
silent, though Beth could feel his small heart hammering
against her own.

She coughed and blinked. Dirt lined her mouth and nose
and clung to her wet dress. She swiped at her eyes with her fist.
If she could just get this dust out of her eyes so she could *see*.

"Annie!" The hoarse croak was almost at her feet. "It's dark!"

The awful truth hit, stunning her like a physical blow. She
willed herself not to reel dizzily in the disorienting absence of

all light, a blackness so intense it felt as if it were crushing her. A scream welled in her throat, but it came out as only a strangled squeak.

"Annie? *Annie?*"

She heard a fresh rattle of falling dirt as Arthur struggled to rise. She tried to rise and found her feet buried in rubble. Fine dirt clogged the air, and another spasm of coughing shook her.

"I—I think the mine tunnel collapsed around us," her voice croaked, sounding alien and unfamiliar. "I think we're... trapped."

Trapped. Her words ricocheted back and forth within her, growing louder and louder until she wanted to pound her ears. Raw claustrophobia sucked at her lungs.

"We aren't trapped!" Arthur cried. "We can dig our way out!"

Dirt flew as Arthur scrabbled desperately at the barrier of earth and broken wood separating them from freedom. Flying clods hit her face and body. With a creak and groan, another weakened section of tunnel crashed down around them.

"Arthur, stop it! Moving a timber started all this. You're going to bring the whole tunnel down on us!"

"What difference does it make?" The once-suave voice now rasped with terror and hysteria. "We're going to die in here anyway!"

Die in here. Beth closed her eyes, the reflex instinctive even if it made no difference; utter blackness with eyes open, utter blackness with eyes shut. Terror. Terror such as she had never known existed. She cringed as another chunk dropped on her from above.

Be calm, she commanded herself fiercely. *The Lord is with us in light or darkness. Even in the collapsed tunnel of an abandoned mine.*

First they must get away from *there,* she knew, where even a strong breath seemed capable of bringing the earth crashing down around them. Holding Joey in one arm, she used her other hand to feel her way along the crumbly wall.

She couldn't tell how far she'd gone…the distance seemed endless in the blackness…before she reached a section that felt more solid, the air not so heavy with dust. When she stopped, Arthur's labored breathing and dragging footsteps told her he had followed.

She slumped to the floor of the tunnel and leaned against the hard wall. Joey snuggled fearfully against her, small arms around her neck. *Oh, Joey, Joey…* The hopelessness of their situation was so overwhelming that she simply held him close and rocked him gently.

"We don't have to wait this out, you know," Arthur rasped from somewhere in the blackness. "We don't have to just sit here and wait for a lingering death."

In spite of all evidence to the contrary, hope blossomed amid Beth's fears. "What do you mean?"

"I have the gun. I found it lying on the backseat beside me after the car went over the edge. There are enough bullets for all of us. We can do it quick and easy."

Beth heard the rustle of fabric, then a metallic click. "No!" she gasped, horrified. "I won't do that. Never!"

"What *are* you going to do?"

She swallowed. "Trust in God."

His snort scorned her answer. "You're going to let Joey suffer? Just sit here in this tomb until lack of food or water kills us? Unless we get lucky and run out of air and suffocate first?"

Until that moment Beth hadn't even thought about the satchel, but mention of food and water reminded her of Joey's needs. Resolutely she simply canceled out everything else

Arthur had just said. She stumbled to her feet and hitched Joey on her hip. She wouldn't leave him with Arthur, not after what he'd said about the gun!

"What are you doing?"

"I'm going to look for the satchel."

Silence, and then Arthur muttered, "I'll do it."

A few minutes later faint scratching sounds echoed back to her as he dug in the rubble for the satchel. Once she heard the crash of more falling earth, followed by a harsh pressure in her ears and a peculiar puff of dirt-laden air rushing by. Then silence again.

She was about to force herself to go back and search for him when she heard dragging noises, and a few minutes later his voice croaked victoriously, "I got it!" just a few feet away from her.

Beth opened the latch with trembling hands, thanking God...and Arthur, too...for the satchel, its contents infinitely more precious than any gold that had ever been found in the mine. Groping inside, she found a can that sloshed when she shook it. Milk for Joey!

"I have a pocketknife to open it," Arthur said. He fumbled the open knife to her in the blackness.

She steadied the can between her knees—although they were none too steady—and punched two holes in the metal top.

"There's water in a glass bottle," Arthur said.

She found the curved bottle. "Do you need a drink?"

"No. You and Joey use it. It won't last long anyway." Echoing unsaid were the words, *And neither will we.*

By feel, Beth mixed the canned milk and water in a baby bottle for Joey. He'd been refusing a bottle lately, preferring a grown-up cup, but he eagerly sucked the milk down now, the noise unnaturally loud in the silence of the tunnel. She removed his wet clothes and bundled him in several diapers to keep him warm; Arthur's foresight had not included bringing other clothes.

Then they simply sat there, Joey asleep in her lap. Beth shivered in her own wet clothes, but the desperate concentration on self-survival released its stranglehold enough to let her thoughts rise outside the tunnel.

Oh, Guy. A wave of almost unbearable longing swept over her. A heart-deep need for him, yet at the same time a thankfulness he wasn't trapped here, too. *I love you! I don't want it to end like this!* She buried herself in the comforting memory of his strong arms around her, the love and passion of his kiss, the lighthearted joy of their laughter. She thought of shared sunshine and rain, shared worship and faith, shared love of Joey. *Oh, Guy!*

"You said Guy was probably following us," Arthur said out of the blackness. "Maybe he'll talk to the old man at the gas station. Maybe the man saw us turn on the side road. Guy will follow it, see the wrecked car, and realize we're trapped in here...."

Arthur's voice ran down like a played-out windup toy as he listed all the "maybes" that would have to occur before Guy could find them. And Beth knew that even those *maybes* were not possible.

"Guy has no idea where we are, and knows nothing about your car. I was just saying that to give myself hope, I suppose."

Hope. And now there was none. They were trapped.

No wedding. No honeymoon. No house on the desert or lifetime sharing of love and joy. No baby brother or sister for Joey. Her eyes closed again, that action which came so naturally in times of pain, even here where it was meaningless.

Yet she could thank the Lord for the sweet, gloriously joyful time of love they had briefly known together. She could thank him, too, that Guy had found his salvation with the Lord.

"And how do you feel about God now?" Arthur's tone was cynical, even as his mind again seemed to follow the path of her own.

"'While I live will I praise the Lord: I will sing praises unto my God while I have any being,'" Beth quoted softly from Psalms.

"He traps you here, abandons you, and you still feel that way?"

"He hasn't abandoned me!" Beth denied fiercely. "I don't like being trapped here. I don't like the idea of dying like this. But I'm not abandoned! I know that even if I die here I'll be with the Lord after this life is over."

Joey stirred in her arms, and she felt the warm trickle of a tear against her cheek. *But Joey... Oh, Lord, please, couldn't you spare him from this harsh and lingering death?*

A new and painful thought occurred to her. What would losing her and Joey do to Guy? Would it destroy his newfound faith? *Oh, Lord, please, NO!* she prayed. *Help him to hold on to his faith no matter what happens to us. Don't let him abandon you because of this.*

"You're not afraid?" Arthur asked skeptically.

"Yes, I'm afraid." She couldn't deny that. The Lord had built into all his living creatures a desperate desire to live. "But I'm not in despair. My grandmother had a saying: 'The length of our time here is merely a nail in the mansion of eternity.' You don't have to be in despair either."

"An old sinner like me?" He laughed. "I'm afraid it'd be a little foolish and hypocritical of me to run whimpering to God at this late date. He'd laugh in my face." He paused reflectively.

"Not that I really believe there's even a God out there to whimper to."

"Yes, there is! And it isn't too late for you to claim the salvation he offers through Jesus! Jesus himself told about the man who early in the morning hired workers for a penny for a day's work. But late in the day the man saw men who still hadn't found work, and he also hired them. And they, too, received their penny the same as those who were hired first. It's the same with salvation: Those who find it late don't receive less than those who come early."

"A penny for a day's work? And we think wages are bad in these depression times," Arthur joked with hollow humor, deliberately ignoring the real message of her words. He sighed. "Annie—no, Bethany… You're a wonderful, courageous, and generous woman. In spite of all I've done to you you're still concerned about my miserable soul. You truly make me ashamed of myself, and I'm sorry I got you involved in this. I'm especially sorry Joey has to suffer for my greed. Your beliefs about God and salvation make a comforting story at a time like this."

"It's not just a comforting story! It's real and true." She paused and took a ragged breath, feeling his stubborn resistance. "Arthur, would you tell me about yourself? Who you really are?"

"What difference does it make now?"

She managed a rueful laugh. "We haven't much else to do." And talking, she knew, would help keep the choking claustrophobia at bay, pushing back the awful terror that the walls were slyly inching closer.

"I suppose that's true," he agreed. He paused, as if considering where to start. "My real name is Arthur Beeman. I was born back in Ohio. I started picking pockets when I was tossed out on my own at age twelve, and I've been a small-time crook ever since. For a while I wanted to be an actor, but, unfortunately, I never had enough talent to get beyond a few walk-on stage parts."

"You had enough talent to deceive me," Beth pointed out wryly.

"Too bad I wasn't that good on stage." He paused reflectively. "You, however, have a genuine talent. Your paintings of children are really quite exceptional."

"How would you know? You're a phony!"

He laughed, a sincere chuckle that sounded strange here with death a silent predator stalking them in the dark. "Actually, I'm quite knowledgeable about art. In recent years I've specialized in handling art forgeries. Rather good quality forgeries, if I do say so myself. It's a fairly gentlemanly occupation."

"Except for this small detour into kidnapping."

"A detour I regret with all my heart."

"Would you have used the gun on me?"

"I like to think I wouldn't have stooped that low. But..." His voice trailed off in the blackness.

"Arthur, will you do one thing for me?"

"There's not much I can do here."

"Will you think about what I said, that it isn't too late to ask Jesus to come into your heart?"

"I suppose I can do that." He laughed wryly. "As you pointed out, there's not much else to do here."

"How did you get involved in Nat Wilkerson's kidnapping scheme?"

"Someone sold him an expensive forgery of a piece of Italian art. An acquaintance put him in touch with me, and I got rid of it for him. When this new...ah...problem came up, he contacted me again. You'd been under surveillance for some time before this complicated plan involving me and a phony art gallery was concocted."

"Where were you taking Joey and me?"

"You weren't supposed to be along. My instructions were to turn Joey over to a woman in Oklahoma City. I think they planned to take him out of the country." He paused and added irrelevantly, "I wonder how many years it will be before our bones are discovered here?"

The question was rhetorical, and Beth did not answer. After a while weariness overtook her. She dozed fitfully. When Joey woke she fed him crackers and applesauce from a can. She took a few bites for herself only because she must be strong enough to care for Joey until…well, *until*. She'd lost all sense of time, and had no idea if it was the middle of the night or morning. Not that it mattered, here where there was no day or night.

"I'm going to see if this tunnel goes anywhere," Arthur said suddenly. "Maybe we're sitting here like hopeless dummies when all we have to do is go around a corner and walk right out the other side."

His clumping steps echoed back for several minutes, but then Beth and Joey were alone in silence. She prayed and dozed and thought about Guy. She sent him wordless messages of love, and held Joey close and dozed and prayed again. She heard Arthur calling her, a dreamlike sensation at first, until she woke and it was real.

"Annie! Where are you?"

"Here!" She guided him with her voice until he reached a trembling hand down to touch her shoulder.

"There are branch tunnels going off this one! The two I followed dead-ended, but—" Tired and shaky as he obviously was, his voice still bubbled with exhilaration. "Annie, I hate to ask, but I need a little water. If I can keep going, maybe I can find a way out!"

Beth didn't know much about mines, but she doubted they usually came with a convenient exit. She handed him the bottle of water and heard him carefully take only a single gulp. *Not a good man,* she thought. *But not all bad, either.*

Again she lost track of time after his footsteps dimmed to silence in the blackness. But this time when he returned he had news.

"I think I've found a way out! I saw stars!"

"Stars?"

"Stars!"

Together they gathered up baby and satchel and groped their way along the tunnel. They came to a side tunnel and passed it. Another branch angled off in the opposite direction, and Arthur bypassed that, too.

"This one," he whispered at the next black opening, as if to speak aloud might make it disappear. "Smell! Doesn't the air smell fresher?"

He grabbed her hand, and she stumbled to keep up as he dragged her along. Yes, the air did smell fresher!

"There!" He blocked her way with an arm. "But stay back."

Above them curved a glimmer of paling sky, and in it…oh, so glorious, so beautiful!…two stars! And the opening was so close!

She pushed forward to get a better look, but again Arthur held her back. "We'll have to wait for daylight. There's a problem, though."

"Problem?" How could there be any significant problem? Freedom was up there, just a few feet away!

"As nearly as I can tell, what we're looking out of is a vertical shaft intersecting this horizontal one. And the vertical one keeps going, straight down. I almost fell into it."

He scratched a rock from the wall of the tunnel and tossed it into the blackness. It seemed a long time before a faint *ping* echoed from the bottom. Beth stepped backward, reeling dizzily at the realization of how easily they all could have plunged into the hole.

"But we'll figure it out when we can see better," Arthur promised.

They sat and waited as the small patch of sky lightened, the stars disappeared, and a faint glow of morning light filtered into their horizontal tunnel. Beth fed Joey, ate a little herself, and got Arthur to take a few strengthening bites. Her clothes were dry, but she was thoroughly chilled. Never, she vowed, was she ever going into another mine tunnel. Never a cave, never a hole in the ground…she'd probably think twice about even entering a basement! She chattered to Joey and helped him toddle back and forth to stretch both his legs and hers, impatiently waiting for Arthur to get started.

Yet, oddly, Arthur didn't seem to share her eagerness. Finally, with Joey tucked in the curve of her arm, she approached him sitting at the edge of the vertical shaft. He didn't speak, just turned and looked at her with a naked despair in his tired eyes.

She looked up, puzzled. The surface was tantalizingly close, not more than four or five feet above the top of their horizontal tunnel. A creosote bush dipped over the rim of the opening, and never had any blooming flower looked as lovely as that plain, dull plant at this moment. Then she looked down, into the shaft plunging into the earth.

And slowly an awful understanding began to dawn.

"I was wrong," he said bleakly. "It isn't a way out."

"Yes, yes it *is!* You can boost me up, hand Joey up to me."

He stood up. "Look again."

She looked. And saw. And knew, even as her mind raged against the deadly truth.

Arthur's head reached to within an inch of the top of their horizontal tunnel. Yet the only way he could boost her up the vertical shaft would be if he were standing where the downward shaft disappeared into the earth. It couldn't be done standing on the edge.

Beth looked upward again. She could see freedom in the blue sky. Hear it in the joyous melody of some desert bird. Smell it in the storm-washed, fresh air. Feel its sweet caress on her skin.

But it was all just an illusion after all.

There was no way out.

Twenty-Two

❧

Guy hung around the police station until after midnight. In spite of promises from both Gillian and Millie to call him instantly if Beth returned home, he telephoned the Gardiner house every few minutes. Then he'd stalk back to confront the officer on duty, with his love and fear for Beth and Joey tangled in a snarl of anger and impatience.

"Surely you can do *something!* Telegraph the police in cities along any route he might take. Set up roadblocks!"

"We're doing what we can. But we don't have much to go on. We don't know what he's driving. We aren't even certain who he is."

"A middle-aged man, with a kidnapped, terrified woman and baby, heading east!" Even as he spoke Guy realized in frustration how vague the description was, how many scores of travelers it undoubtedly fit.

"We don't even know a crime has been committed," the officer pointed out patiently. "Usually a kidnapper wants ransom."

"The man behind this isn't after a ransom." How could he begin to explain Nat Wilkerson's obsession with controlling his grandson?

"She may even have gone with him willingly. Women do strange things sometimes." The officer launched into a lurid story about a young wife who ran off with her best friend's father.

Guy turned away, not waiting to hear the end of the story. Beth hadn't run off willingly! But even in his frustration he could understand the police point of view; they had only his claim that there had been an abduction, no proof.

He went home, read his Bible, and raged over and over as he paced the floor, "Lord, show me what to do!" He tried to grab some sleep, but between fragmented dreams and tossing and turning, stumbled out of bed at daybreak feeling as if he'd spent the night on a battlefield. Unmindful of the time, he called the Gardiner house. Millie checked Beth's room, just in case she'd slipped in unnoticed in the night, but reported that it was still untouched and empty.

Lord, tell me what to do! I have to do something now!

He went by the police station again, then to the *Courier.* He scheduled a boxed notice headed MISSING—POSSIBLE ABDUCTION on the front page. By midafternoon, when he'd still heard nothing, he grimly made a decision; one man knew exactly where they were and what was going on. He placed the phone call, fist beating the desk in impatience as the operators plodded through the slow process of long-distance connections. He didn't recognize the young female voice that answered. New secretary?

"Mr. Wilkerson, please," Guy said. "Nat Wilkerson."

"May I tell him who's calling?"

He wasn't going to give Nat the chance to have the secretary brush him off with some phony "in conference" or "out of town" garbage. "Mike Randolph," he invented on the spot. "It's about a real estate deal he's interested in." He knew how to snag Nat.

Several moments of silence, then, "Hello."

Once that strong, self-confident voice commanded his respect and admiration. No more. "Hello, Father."

What did he expect? Anger? Explanations? A claim of ignorance? What he got was simply an arrogant click as Nat hung up on him.

Angrily he jiggled the phone. He started to place another call, then abruptly decided against it. He had a better idea.

He put the competent, hard-working society editor in charge of the newspaper, studied a map briefly, and returned to his apartment just long enough to throw a few things into a suitcase.

The miles whipped by under the heavy pressure of his foot on the accelerator, the high-powered Packard roaring around slower-moving vehicles as if they were lumbering oxen from out of the past. The dark cliffs of the Superstitions rose flat and featureless under a sky bleached to faded denim by blaze of sun.

Arthur had to be taking Beth and Joey to Nat in St. Louis, Guy reasoned. He mentally played with various rescue schemes, some legal, some not so legal. He explored confrontation, threats, even a dark vengeance. Maybe he could get to St. Louis before Arthur did, perhaps even intercept them on the way. If not… His hands clamped the steering wheel accompanied by a savage urge to do the same to Nat's throat.

But alone out here on the desert, surrounded by endless stretches of harsh earth and cactuses, with a hot wind searing his face, the deadly fear he'd been avoiding slammed into him like the windshield of the Packard smashing into some helpless desert bug.

Maybe he was already too late.

Joey was relatively safe, at least physically, he was reasonably certain. Joey was the target and object of all this. But Beth? Beth was undoubtedly expendable in Nat's arrogant, self-centered scheme.

His foot weakened on the accelerator at the thought, then abruptly crashed to the brake pedal at sight of something lying alongside the road up ahead. A body? *Please, Lord, no!*

The Packard skidded to a stop scarcely inches from the bundle of old burlap bags fallen from some passing truck. Guy dropped his head between hands gone nerveless on the steering wheel.

Yet it could have been Beth…. He lifted his head and stared helplessly at the cactus-strewn desert cut with rough gullies and washes. There were a million hiding places out there where a body might never be found.

Beth, Beth, I love you.

His own inability to help Beth suddenly washed over him like a suffocating nightmare. Oh, his incredible arrogance, he thought as his own words thundered back at him. *He* would protect and take care of Beth and Joey, he had proudly proclaimed. *He* wouldn't let Nat harm them or take Joey. Beth and Joey would be safe with *him*.

He had turned his eternal life over to God, but he was still stubbornly claiming he could handle *this* life on his own, subconsciously clinging to an arrogant self-sufficiency and the old feeling that it was a show of weakness to depend on God. Show *me* what to do, he had imperiously demanded. *I* will save her. He had put his trust in the Lord for the life beyond this one, but he hadn't yet put his full trust in him in this life. He had made his commitment; he believed in the Lord. But still he clung to that stubborn and prideful trait of humanity, the "I can do it myself" mentality. Believing the fact of salvation was somehow different from putting your whole trust and faith in the

Lord, of letting go and depending on him.

With raw honesty Guy now faced what he *couldn't* do. He couldn't protect Beth from the evil of Rafferty's deadly plans or impulses; he couldn't keep Joey out of Nat's clutches. He couldn't even be certain, he realized raggedly, that Arthur was taking Beth and Joey to St. Louis; Nat may have some other destination in mind for them, beyond Guy's reach, beyond reach of the law.

But not, he thought slowly, beyond God's reach. He straightened in the seat, damp hands sticking to the leather-covered steering wheel. *Everything* was within God's reach.

What could he do? By and of himself, nothing. But he could put his trust where it belonged, not in himself but in the Lord. He closed his eyes and the words of a Psalm came to him: *Be still, and know that I am God.*

He stayed there beside the road for long minutes, praying and communing with the Lord, asking for his strength and compassion in caring for and protecting Beth and Joey. He asked for courage and wisdom for Beth, safety for both of them, wisdom and good judgment for himself. And when he finally returned to the road he drove in the peaceful calm of knowing he had turned everything over to the Lord. And he could now ask, "What would you have me do, Lord?" with the submission of obedience, not demand.

Some miles farther on he passed a faded sign advertising gas, eats, and groceries, and a couple of miles beyond stood a weathered building with a gas pump out front. His foot let up on the gas pedal as he remembered he'd eaten nothing today but a hurried cup of coffee and doughnut at his desk. But more important than that was the possibility someone here may have spotted Arthur and Beth.

An old man with a cane limped out to the pumps, and

behind him an equally slow-moving hound. Guy asked his question: Had the man seen a middle-aged man, very pretty young woman with striking auburn hair, and a blond baby?

"Yep." The old man nodded. "They was some folks like that come through yesterday afternoon. Man and his daughter and grandson. Nice folks. Kin o' your'n?"

"Were they...okay?"

"Well, the daughter had a twisted wrist or somethin'. Seemed a mite edgy, now that I think of it," the old man added reflectively.

Guy clenched his jaw. If Arthur Rafferty had hurt her— He cut off that harsh thought with another: Beth was, at least at this point yesterday, alive. "Where did they go?"

The old man chuckled. "Ain't but two ways to go from here." He raised a bony finger. "They was headed that way."

Guy followed the direction of that pointing finger and settled into the leather seat for an all-night drive. By the time he glanced in the rearview mirror the weathered old building had faded into the desert landscape.

Twenty-Three

❧

Beth sat a few feet back in the tunnel, away from the dark hole of the vertical shaft. She fed Joey. They played a lively game of finding fingers and noses as she determinedly kept her fears from exploding through her fragile shell of control, terrifying Joey. Despite the bluish tinge of several bruises and a few scratches, he seemed untouched by what he'd been through. Although a new word had come into his small vocabulary, a new word describing something he didn't like. *Dark*.

A glow of sunshine crept down the side of the vertical shaft as the sun rose higher in the sky. Arthur spent most of his time sitting with his feet dangling into the shaft, a position incongruously like that of some rich man lolling at the edge of his swimming pool.

When he got up and disappeared into the tunnel, Beth didn't question why. She wearily wanted to sleep, but Joey was awake and curiously investigating everything. Beth knew she dare not doze and risk having him tumble into that hole.

Yet she realized she'd definitely dozed when a strange noise rumbled from the depths of the tunnel. Another cave-in? No, no, please, she couldn't stand any more of that.

She jumped up in astonishment as Arthur appeared, sweat running down his face, dragging a dark timber behind him. He stopped and mopped his face with a dirty shirttail.

"I'm not sure it's long enough."

"Long enough for what?" Hope rose in her even as his intentions puzzled her.

"To lay across the vertical shaft."

"What good will that do?" Beth cried in disappointment. "We're just as trapped on the other side as we are on this one!"

"No, we don't go to the other side. We lay the timber across the hole. I stand on it. You climb on my shoulders and I boost you and Joey to the surface."

Beth's gaze darted from timber to dark shaft to the near-yet-so-far surface just a few feet above them. She mentally measured Arthur's height, added hers to it, measured them both against the barrier of distance.

Arthur's gaze followed hers. "I don't know," he admitted. "Will it work?"

Together they struggled awkwardly with the treacherously slivery old timber. It was too heavy for them simply to lift and fling across the hole like a board. Beth used her weight to balance the back end, at the same time doing what she could to help Arthur shove the timber forward. With a final heave it went. Arthur's arms windmilled wildly for balance, and Beth frantically grabbed his shirt to pull him back before he took a tumble over the edge.

"You did it!" she said. The timber bridged the shaft with not more than a couple of inches to spare on each side. But it was enough!

"*We* did it. Now…" He slid to a sitting position, as much to still his shaking limbs as to snatch a moment's rest, Beth knew.

245

"Have you ever had any desire to be a circus performer?" he inquired after his breathing slowed to a semblance of normal.

A peculiar question, she thought. "Not really. Why?"

"Because I think a bit of trapeze or tightwire talent would be useful here." He paused. "To say nothing of a few powerful prayers."

Beth's almost empty stomach tightened into a rawhide knot as Arthur explained his plans in detail, and she realized clearly how perilous and questionable his plan was. She looked again at the timber spanning the vertical shaft, and it shrank to pencil thinness compared to the yawning emptiness on either side. Arthur must balance on that, and *she* must balance on his shoulders.

Slick perspiration flooded her hands, and she wrapped her arms around Joey, much to his annoyance because he was busily scooping bits of rock into a pile.

"I could try to drag up another timber to make a wider base to stand on, but I'm not sure I'd have the strength left to lift you."

Beth could see he was already approaching near-exhaustion, absentmindedly massaging the arthritic leg. She pressed a sip of water on him. "I could try to drag another one."

"No. You're going to need all your strength to get you and Joey out. And we can't waste time. We're almost out of water." He wiped his hands on his pants and stood up. "I'll go out on it alone first."

He stepped on the end of the timber, one hand over his head to keep contact with the rocky wall of the vertical shaft as he tested the timber for strength, the other hand splayed in empty air for balance. He did it twice for practice, then said, "Hand me your shoes."

"My shoes!" But she did as he requested, and then watched

as he sailed them up and out of the shaft. She heard reassuring thuds as each shoe landed on solid ground somewhere out of sight. They smiled at each other. One small success!

He came back to solid ground and rested a few more minutes, gathering strength for the tests of will and physical endurance to come.

"Will you pray with me?" Beth asked softly. When he didn't answer, she touched his shoulder lightly. "I'll pray for both of us."

When she had finished, he stood up. "One more thing. With luck...and God's help," he conceded with a faint smile, "you and Joey will get out. Then you'll have to hike out to bring back help. I know I don't deserve it, but *will* you come back?"

"Yes! Of course I will. I couldn't abandon you here!"

He surveyed her with tired eyes, eyes in which she saw the weight of mistakes made, wrong paths chosen, disappointments with himself and others. He nodded, more to himself than her. "Yes, I believe you will come back." Then his voice turned brisk and businesslike, and he bent to one knee on the ground. "Okay, this is it. Start out kneeling on my shoulders. Then, when we get out on the timber, stand up."

Of trapeze or tightwire talent she had none. But prayers she had aplenty, and she used them in nonstop pleas for strength, courage...and balance! She thought of that long-ago photograph taken with her girlhood friends, caught in a frivolous moment of human pyramid building—three girls on bottom, two on their shoulders, Beth herself on top, arms joyously outflung in triumph.

This was no different than that, she assured herself as Arthur knelt and Beth, Joey clutched firmly in one arm, awkwardly climbed on his shoulders. She tangled her free hand in his hair, knees on his shoulders, thighs pressed against his head. She gave no thought to the impropriety of the position; her desire for survival canceled out such details.

Arthur half rose and edged bent-backed onto the timber.

With awful clarity she remembered the moment *after* the photograph was taken, when all six girls crashed to the ground, laughing and happy. But here there was no soft green grass to catch her.

She thought of Guy, and winged messages of love out to him—maybe the last such messages she could ever send.

Oh, don't look down! she commanded herself fiercely as she slowly straightened. *Don't look down!*

Arthur turned and steadied himself with both hands against the wall of the vertical shaft. There was nothing for him to clutch, no handhold to grab…but there were Beth's prayers, and she never let go of them.

And now, as she curled one bare foot and then the other into the muscle and bone of Arthur's shoulders, she was grateful for his foresight in getting rid of the stiff impediment of her shoes. She knew she must be close to yanking his hair out by the roots, but he made no complaint.

Joey wiggled in the clutch of her arm, and she planted a swift kiss on his head. "Don't squirm, sweetie. Please don't squirm."

Slowly, indeed like some desperately novice high-wire walker, she loosed her grip on Arthur's hair and eased the palm of her hand up the wall and straightened her back. *Don't lean back,* she willed herself. *Slowly, slowly….*

Then she couldn't help a cry of joy as her gaze slipped over the rim. "I can see out!"

Her gaze took in a barren, desolate land, with no sign of human life anywhere, except for her shoes! There they lay, like small magic carpets awaiting her.

"Can you get Joey out?" Arthur asked.

She felt a sagging shudder run through his body and into her bare feet, but then he steadied himself, straightening and giving her another inch or two.

She had to lean her shoulder against the wall, work Joey into a position with his little legs around her neck. "Okay, I'm going to push you now," she whispered to him. "Don't be scared. You may tumble a bit, but you'll be fine."

She knew the words were beyond Joey's understanding, but she entrusted him to the Lord, as with a grunt and shove she pushed him over her head.

He howled as he hit the hard earth and rolled like a small tumbleweed. Beth knew what would happen as soon as he got his baby wits collected. He'd come toddling back to her. She had to get out before then.

"Give me a shove!" she gasped.

She felt Arthur's hands squeeze between the soles of her feet and his shoulders, then give her a mighty heave.

She scrambled upward, unmindful of cutting rocks and sandpaper earth, battling for every fraction of an inch. Arthur's hands followed her feet as they left his shoulders, giving her every ounce of support he had. Almost there, almost—

The support collapsed.

A scream…a nightmare scream of terror!

She hung there, feet dangling, knees scraping the hard wall as the scream fell away beneath her. Even after she knew it ended, she still heard it, echoing on and on, until she no longer knew if it came from outside or within her. And then she felt herself slipping.

Frantically she kicked, scrabbled with her knees, dug in with elbows. A shower of small rocks rattled past her. Then, arms outstretched, Joey toddled forward.

"No! Joey, don't! Stay back!"

Desperately she flung every ounce of strength into one last effort, straining muscle and bone, lungs and prayer. Oh, yes, prayer! She clawed with knees and toes, elbows, hands, fingers, fingernails! If she could just reach that creosote bush.

She wrapped her fingers around a few leaves...her other hand around a small branch...knee over the edge... And then, almost as if the Lord himself gave her a boost, her body spilled over the top.

She lay there weakly, almost disbelieving, the sun like a warm blessing on her back.

"Mama, mama, mama! Hurt!"

Joey plopped down beside her, face streaked with dirty rivulets of tears, and showed her the skinned places on his legs and fingers.

She wrapped her arms around him and rocked him back and forth to comfort them both. "Yes, sweetie, I know you're hurt."

She was too, she realized. Her knees looked like some poor-grade hamburger, and when Joey touched her nose his finger came away bloody.

Carefully she carried Joey to a safe place some twenty feet from the unmarked hole and sternly told him to stay there. Then she returned to the shaft, lay flat on her stomach, and peered downward. She could see nothing, hear nothing, just silence and a dark descent into awful emptiness. She knew, however, that it wasn't empty now.

But Arthur wasn't necessarily dead. He could be lying at the bottom, injured. Help, she must get help!

Frantically she gathered her shoes and slipped them on her feet. How far was it back to the main road and that gas station?

Regretfully she thought of the satchel trapped in the tunnel, and the food and remaining sips of water it contained. But there was no time for regrets now.

She took a few moments to orient herself toward the rising sun, the direction she thought they'd traveled on the old road, and her guess as to the underground lay of the tunnel. Then she settled Joey on her hip, offered another prayer for guidance, and started off in what she hoped was the direction of the old road.

The going was up-and-down rough, her mouth already drying, but vegetation was sparse so she didn't have to fight her way through a tangle of cactus. She remembered hearing somewhere that it was possible to get water from certain cactuses, but she had no idea which ones nor any way to get at it.

Yet…water! She stared at the tiny pool collected in a crevice of rock from yesterday's storm, halfway certain it was some tiny mirage. But when she fell to her knees beside it and scooped a handful into her mouth, it was real water.

"Oh, Joey; look, look!" She lifted a handful to his mouth and felt the joy of discovered treasure in the delight of his wet smile.

Together they drank the tiny pool of a few cupfuls dry, and just over the next rise found the road. Yesterday it had looked nearly impassable; today it was a superhighway to civilization!

Yet civilization, she found as she trudged on and on, still seemed little closer hours later. The sun grew hotter; now it was overhead, rather than behind her, and then she was walking toward it as it arced slowly across the sky. She had to carry Joey most of the time, although she put him down frequently to toddle a few steps on his own. The pain in the hand that had ached from the crush of Arthur's heel yesterday was no more than background static among the fresh pains of this day: the rub of shoe leather on heel, aching arms and shoulders from Joey's weight, raw knees.

She ripped a section from her skirt to shade Joey, another section to shade her own face. Whenever she found a bit of shadow cast by rock or bush she wearily stopped to rest. She actually saw a mirage once, a great pool of shimmering water, so real she almost felt she could dive into it.

But the Lord supplied their need for water. Not a generous supply, she thought wryly as she actually licked the last drops out of a tiny pocket in the rock. But enough.

Finally, yes! She could look out and see the flatter plain of desert below. And that speck in the distance, with a faint glitter of glass out front…the gas station! She could even see a couple of vehicles, play cars on a play road. But moving, moving because *people* were driving them!

More trudging, more rests, more prayers and thanks.

Then, she recognized this place! It was the jumble of boulders Arthur had hidden the car behind when he first pulled off the road. Her mind told her legs to run. They were almost to help and safety! But her tired feet could do no more than plod onward.

The main road.

The gas station.

The friendly tan hound ambled out to meet them with skinny tail wagging. The door opened as she reached for it. The old man stared at her in astonishment.

"Why, miss. What in the world happened to you?"

The sound of a car pulling up to the gas pump. Beth turned her head to look only because the hound bumped into her.

And she saw the most glorious mirage she'd seen yet this day, the most glorious mirage, she knew, that she'd ever see.

"Beth?" Guy blinked, disbelieving at sight of the drooping, bedraggled, bruised, and sunburned figure in the doorway. Her torn skirt revealed raw knees, and a rag over her head shaded scratched face and scabbed nose. But in spite of her exhaustion she carried the baby in her arms as if she were prepared to go a thousand miles with him. And Guy had never seen a more beautiful sight. "Beth!"

They stared, neither quite able to believe that the other was really there.

She turned to him…no, collapsed against him, and he enfolded both of them in his arms. He dropped kisses on Beth's bent head, murmured words of love and comfort and silently thanked the Lord again and again for whatever he had done to bring them, obviously battered both mentally and physically, but safe…safe!…back to him. The old man stood in the open door, obviously astonished by the reunion of this strange trio in his little store. He disappeared and returned with water, which Beth gratefully gave first to Joey and then gulped herself.

Guy didn't ask questions, even though a hundred of them flooded his mind. Now all that mattered was food and rest and medical attention.

Yet when Beth lifted her head it wasn't food or rest for which she asked. "I have to go back," she whispered.

"Back? Back *where?*"

A fantastic story tumbled out of her. Abduction, wrecked car, collapsed mine shaft. As she talked, Guy led her inside to a bench, the little he already knew dovetailing with the strange tale. Rafferty's accomplice, he realized, must have decided, when his kidnapping target was missing, simply to burglarize the house. He snuggled Joey in one arm and kept the other arm wrapped tightly around Beth's shoulders.

253

"Arthur's still down there," she finally gasped raggedly. "I promised I'd bring back help to get him out."

A fall down a mine shaft. Hours since the fall. There wasn't a chance in this world that he was still alive. Guy cut off the thought that the man got what he deserved. Judgment was God's arena, not his.

"You're in no shape to go anywhere," he said flatly.

"I have to! I have to show you where it is."

"I know where that old shaft is," the old man interrupted. He had been unabashedly listening to every word of Beth's incredible story. "I did a little prospectin' up there myself, in my younger days."

Guy glanced out the dust-specked window at the slanting shafts of sinking sun. "Can we get there before dark?"

"Maybe. If'n we step on it. We can go in my old truck."

Guy didn't want to do this. He didn't want to leave Beth and Joey for even an instant. Yet one look into Beth's tired, troubled face told him he had to do it.

He and the old man settled Beth and Joey in the living quarters adjoining the store. The old man waved toward the tiny kitchen and told her to help herself to anything she wanted. He stuck a "Closed" sign on the outside door and went to gather the gear they'd need.

Guy wrapped his arms around Beth again, and she rested her head on his chest. Weary little Joey had already fallen asleep on the sofa.

"How did you get here?" Beth asked. She sat a little straighter as if only then aware of the unlikelihood of what had just happened. "How did we both get here at the same time?"

Guy smiled and brushed a drooping lock of hair behind her ear. Even a layer of dust could not hide the auburn glow. "Do you really need to ask?"

She managed a smile, too, although her eyes had a giveaway shine of tears. "No, I don't think I do."

"I was headed for St. Louis. I stopped here to ask about you and went on. But I got a few miles down the road, decided I'd better fill up with gas, and turned back."

"God turned you back."

Yes. Although it was not the only thing God had done with him these last few hours. Sometimes God brought his stumbling, stubborn people to the point where they *must* depend on him. He thanked the Lord again for answering his frantic, fervent prayers for care and protection for both Beth and Joey.

"I love you," Beth whispered. "For a while I was afraid I'd never get to tell you that again."

"I love you. And I had the same fear." He kissed her again, and then followed the store's proprietor out to the truck.

At the suggestion of the old man, Riley Higgins, they drove a few miles out of the way to enlist help. Some of Guy's doubts about this rescue attempt relaxed when he saw Mike McAndrews, a six-foot, two-hundred-and-twenty pound hunk of good-humored muscle who was eking out a sparse living on a mining claim of his own.

As Guy suspected, however, this was not a rescue; he was not surprised at what he found when the other two men lowered him on a rope into the shaft.

It was dark by the time they got back to the gas station. A lantern Beth had lit still burned, but she was asleep on the sofa, her body curled around Joey's.

Guy looked down at them, his heart overflowing with love and gratitude. In sleep, each bruise and wound stood out on her skin, the faint half-circles beneath her eyes more than mere shadows of the fringe of her eyelashes. Even her hand, tucked protectively around Joey, was raw and swollen.

He slipped his arms beneath her, hoping he could carry her to the car without waking her, but her eyes flew open.

"Arthur?" she asked.

"Dead. Instantly, I think." In the glare of a flashlight at the bottom of the shaft, where he had an inkling of the claustrophobic horror of Beth's entrapment in the tunnel, he hadn't needed a doctor's expertise to recognize the impossible angle of Arthur's head as a broken neck.

A fleeting pain crossed her face, and she shook her head as if in protest. "We never know when it's going to be too late, do we?"

The question didn't seem to require an answer, at least none he could give, so all he said was, "We brought his body out."

"Thank you," she whispered.

He'd intended to carry her and Joey separately to the car, but when she tensed, hand clutching frantically for the baby, he snuggled Joey right on top of her and felt her drowsily relax.

Guy relaxed too, because he had them both now, right next to his heart. Where they belonged.

Twenty-Four

❧

Beth removed her paint-stained smock when she spied the flag of dust on the road. She ran her fingers lightly through her hair. The auburn waves still weren't as long as they had once been, but they curled softly almost to her shoulders now. Fireball Joey, in the midst of his terrible two's, raced for the door yelling, "Daddy, Daddy, Daddy!" His equally rambunctious puppy ran behind him, both of them skidding and squealing around corners like miniature fire engines.

Guy swooped Joey up in one arm and wrapped the other around Beth. The puppy yapped, Joey chattered about the lizard he'd found, and Kate Smith warbled from the radio in the kitchen, the sound accompanied by the tantalizing scent of freshly baked bread. Guy grinned happily at this small pandemonium that greeted him each day.

"What do I get for some fantastic news?" he asked.

"That depends. How fantastic? Has our new refrigerator come in?"

"Yes. But this is better news than that. Much better."

Beth thought hard. God had been so good to them, and so many wonderful things had happened already! The newspaper was prospering. After months of delay, electricity now brightened the house and made life easier. She'd sold another painting last week. Gillian's marriage was holding together, and Ariana wrote little letters regularly.

And, after her trip to town today, Beth had some rather exciting news of her own! But all she said now was, "I give up. Tell me," and reached up to bribe him with a kiss on his teasing smile.

"This news deserves more than one kiss."

She planted a wild flurry of kisses on smile and cheeks, and Joey contributed exuberant kisses for both of them. Guy set Joey on the bright Navajo rug, and with a flourish produced an important-looking document from the inner pocket of his jacket. Beth snatched the stiff fold of paper. It couldn't be…could it? The lawyer had said it might take several months yet.

"The lawyer phoned, and I picked it up this afternoon. Joey's adoption papers."

Joey played happily with his puppy, oblivious to removal of this threat that had hung over all of them for so long. Beth pressed the precious document to her chest, her throat tight with emotion.

"He's legally ours now." Guy dipped his forehead to hers and offered a husky prayer of thanks, for they both knew that without the Lord's help they could never have defeated the avalanche of high-powered lawyers, money and influence Nat had thrown at them in the battle over Joey.

Then Beth lifted her head with shining eyes. "Don't stop the thanks there." Her smile was both tremulous and a bit mischievous. She touched her waist lightly, where only the faintest of bulges revealed the secret within. "I saw the doctor today, and I have some news too."

Guy's whoop of joy for this second special gift from God echoed from adobe house to desert hilltop…and beyond.

258

Dear Reader

I've been curious. Do readers read our author letters before or after they read the story? I've wondered if you read an author's letter to find out what the story is about...or to find out about the author after you've read the story?

So, if you're reading this before you read the story, I'll just tell you that it's about Beth Curtis, who has, with both joy and sadness, taken on the responsibility of raising her baby nephew, and Guy Wilkerson, member of the rich and powerful family that ruthlessly wants to take the baby from her. And that the title, *Escape*, has a dual meaning that I hope you'll find both exciting and meaningful.

If you are reading this letter after you've finished the book, to find out about the person who wrote about these people, I can tell you that I am a Christian, a wife, a mother, and a writer. I always start my writing day by reading a chapter or two of Scripture and asking for the Lord's help and guidance in writing. I know I often fall short in what the Lord would have me accomplish, but I keep trying. I also enjoy writing a good deal more than I do housework, which is the reason you may find dust on my coffee table or dishes in need of washing at my home. Fortunately, my husband takes a tolerant attitude toward this, and I hope the Lord does also.

I received such nice letters after my earlier Palisades novel, *Betrayed*, was published, and I've tried to answer them all. Thank you so much for writing.

Lorena McCourtney

Lorena McCourtney, c/o Palisades
P.O. Box 1720, Sisters, Oregon 97759

PALISADES...PURE ROMANCE

⁓ PALISADES ⁓

Reunion, Karen Ball
Refuge, Lisa Tawn Bergren
Torchlight, Lisa Tawn Bergren
Treasure, Lisa Tawn Bergren
Chosen, Lisa Tawn Bergren
Firestorm, Lisa Tawn Bergren (October, 1996)
Cherish, Constance Colson
Angel Valley, Peggy Darty
Seascape, Peggy Darty
Sundance, Peggy Darty
Love Song, Sharon Gillenwater
Antiques, Sharon Gillenwater
Secrets, Robin Jones Gunn
Whispers, Robin Jones Gunn
Echoes, Robin Jones Gunn
Coming Home, Barbara Jean Hicks
Glory, Marilyn Kok
Sierra, Shari MacDonald
Forget-Me-Not, Shari MacDonald
Diamonds, Shari MacDonald (November, 1996)
Westward, Amanda MacLean
Stonehaven, Amanda MacLean
Everlasting, Amanda MacLean
Betrayed, Lorena McCourtney
Escape, Lorena McCourtney
Voyage, Elaine Schulte

A Christmas Joy, Darty, Gillenwater, MacLean
Mistletoe, Ball, Hicks, McCourtney (October, 1996)

THE PALISADES LINE

Reunion, Karen Ball
ISBN 0-88070-951-0
There are wolves on Taylor Sorensen's ranch. Wildlife biologist Connor Alexander is sure of it. So he takes a job as a ranch hand to prove it. Soon he and Taylor are caught in a fierce controversy—and in a determined battle against the growing attraction between them...an attraction that neither can ignore.

Chosen, Lisa Tawn Bergren
ISBN 0-88070-768-2
When biblical archeologist Alexsana Rourke is handed the unprecedented honor of excavating Solomon's Stables in Jerusalem, she has no idea that she'll need to rely heavily upon the new man in her life—CNN correspondent Ridge McIntyre—and God, to save her.

Refuge, Lisa Tawn Bergren
ISBN 0-88070-875-1 (New ISBN)
Part One: A Montana rancher and a San Francisco marketing exec—only one incredible summer and God could bring such diverse lives together. *Part Two:* Lost and alone, Emily Walker needs and wants a new home, a sense of family. Can one man lead her to the greatest Father she could ever want and a life full of love?

Firestorm, Lisa Tawn Bergren (October, 1996)
ISBN 0-88070-953-7
In the sequel to Bergren's best-selling *Refuge, Firestorm* tells the romantic tale of two unlikely soulmates: a woman who fears fire, and the man who loves it. Reyne Oldre wasn't always afraid, but a tragic accident one summer changed her forever. Can Reyne get beyond her fear and give her heart to smoke jumper Logan McCabe?

Torchlight, Lisa Tawn Bergren
ISBN 0-88070-806-9
When beautiful heiress Julia Rierdon returns to Maine to remodel her family's estate, she finds herself torn between the man she plans to marry and unexpected feelings for a mysterious wanderer who threatens to steal her heart.

Treasure, Lisa Tawn Bergren
ISBN 0-88070-725-9
She arrived on the Caribbean island of Robert's Foe armed with a lifelong dream—to find her ancestor's sunken ship—and yet the only man who can help her stands stubbornly in her way. Can Christina and Mitch find their way to the ship *and* to each other?

Cherish, Constance Colson
ISBN 0-88070-802-6
Recovering from the heartbreak of a failed engagement, Rose Anson seeks refuge at a resort on Singing Pines Island, where she plans to spend a peaceful summer studying and painting the spectacular scenery of international Lake of the Woods. But when a flamboyant Canadian and a big-hearted American compete for her love, the young artist must face her past—and her future. What follows is a search for the source and meaning of true love: a journey that begins in the heart and concludes in the soul.

Angel Valley, Peggy Darty
ISBN 0-88070-778-X
When teacher Laurel Hollingsworth accepts a summer tutoring position for a wealthy socialite family, she faces an enormous challenge in her young student, Anna Lee Wentworth. However, the real challenge is ahead of her: hanging on to her heart when older brother Matthew Wentworth comes to visit. Soon Laurel and Matthew find that they share a faith in God...and powerful feelings for one another. Can Laurel and Matthew find time to explore their relationship while she helps the emotionally troubled Anna Lee and fights to defend her love for the beautiful *Angel Valley*?

Seascape, Peggy Darty
ISBN 0-88070-927-8
On a pristine sugar sand beach in Florida, Jessica has a lot to reflect upon. The untimely death of her husband, Blake...and the sudden entrance of a new man, distracting her from her grief. In the midst of opening a B&B, can Jessica overcome her anger and forgive the one responsible for Blake's death? Loving the mysterious new man in her life will depend upon it.

Sundance, Peggy Darty
ISBN 0-88070-952-9
Follow Ginger Grayson to the wilds of British Columbia, Canada, where she meets Craig Cameron, a widowed rancher with two small sons who desperately need a mother. Is free-spirited Ginger ready to settle down in the 1990's last wild frontier? And can Craig risk his heart again, all the while wondering if Ginger can handle his rugged lifestyle?

Love Song, Sharon Gillenwater
ISBN 0-88070-747-X
When famous country singer Andrea Carson returns to her hometown to recuperate from a life-threatening illness, she seeks nothing more than a respite from the demands of stardom that have sapped her creativity and ability to perform. It's Andi's old high school friend, Wade Jamison, who helps her to realize that she needs inner healing as well. As Andi's strength grows, so do her feelings for the rancher who has captured her heart. But can their relationship withstand the demands of her career? Or will their romance be as fleeting as a beautiful *Love Song*?

Antiques, Sharon Gillenwater
ISBN 0-88070-801-8
Deeply wounded by the infidelity of his wife, widower Grant Adams swore off all women—until meeting charming antiques dealer Dawn Carson. Although he is drawn to her, Grant struggles to trust again. Dawn finds herself overwhelmingly attracted to the darkly brooding cowboy, but won't marry a nonbeliever. As Grant learns more about her faith, he is touched by its impact on her life and slowly begins to trust.

Echoes, Robin Jones Gunn
ISBN 0-88070-773-9
In this dramatic romance filled with humor, Lauren Phillips enters the wild, uncharted territory of the Internet on her home computer and "connects" with a man known only as "KC." Recovering from a broken engagement and studying for her teaching credential, her correspondence with KC becomes the thing she enjoys most. Will their e-mail romance become a true love story when they meet face to face?

Secrets, Robin Jones Gunn
ISBN 0-88070-721-6
Seeking a new life as an English teacher in a peaceful Oregon town, Jessica tries desperately to hide the details of her identity from the community...until she falls in love. Will the past keep Jessica and Kyle apart forever?

Whispers, Robin Jones Gunn
ISBN 0-88070-755-0
Teri Moreno went to Maui eager to rekindle a romance. But when circumstances turn out to be quite different than she expects, she finds herself spending a great deal of time with a handsome, old high school crush who now works at a local resort. But the situation becomes more complicated when Teri meets Gordon, a clumsy, endearing Australian with a wild past, and both men begin to pursue her. Will Teri respond to God's gentle urgings toward true love? The answer lies in her response to the gentle *Whispers* in her heart.

Coming Home, Barbara Hicks
ISBN 0-88070-945-6

Keith Castle is running from a family revelation that destroyed his world, and deeply hurt his heart. Katie Brannigan is the childhood friend who was wounded by his sudden disappearance. Together, Keith and Katie could find healing and learn that in his own time, God manages all things for good. But can Katie bring herself to give love one more chance?

Glory, Marilyn Kok
ISBN 0-88070-754-2

To Mariel Forrest, the teaching position in Taiwan provided more than a simple escape from grief; it also offered an opportunity to deal with her feelings toward the God she once loved, but ultimately blamed for the death of her family. Once there, Mariel dares to ask the timeless question: "If God is good, why do we suffer?" What follows is an inspiring story of love, healing, and renewed confidence in God's goodness.

Diamonds, Shari MacDonald (November, 1996)
ISBN 0-88070-982-0

When spirited sportscaster Casey Foster inherits a minor league team, she soon discovers that baseball isn't all fun and games. Soon, Casey is juggling crazy promotional events, major league expectations, and egos of players like Tucker Boyd: a pitcher who wants nothing more than to return to the major leagues...until Casey captures his heart and makes him see diamonds in a whole new way.

Forget-Me-Not, Shari MacDonald
ISBN 0-88070-769-0

Traveling to England's famed Newhaven estate to pursue an internship as a landscape architect, Hayley Buckman looked forward to making her long-held career dreams come true. But upon arrival, Hayley is quickly drawn to the estate and its mysterious inhabitants, despite a sinister warning urging her to leave. Will an endearing stranger help her solve the mystery and find love as well?

Sierra, Shari MacDonald
ISBN 0-88070-726-7

When spirited photographer Celia Randall travels to eastern California for a short-term assignment, she quickly is drawn to—and locks horns with—editor Marcus Stratton. Will lingering heartaches destroy Celia's chance at true love? Or can she find hope and healing high in the *Sierra*?

Westward, Amanda MacLean

Running from a desperate fate in the South toward an unknown future in the West, plantation-born artist Juliana St. Clair finds herself torn between two men, one an undercover agent with a heart of gold, the other a man with evil intentions and a smooth facade. Witness Juliana's dangerous travels toward faith and love as she follows God's lead in this powerful historical novel.

Stonehaven, Amanda MacLean
ISBN 0-88070-757-7

Picking up in the years following *Westward*, *Stonehaven* follows Callie St. Clair back to the South where she has returned to reclaim her ancestral home. As she works to win back the plantation, the beautiful and dauntless Callie turns it into a station on the Underground Railroad. Covering her actions by playing the role of a Southern belle, Callie risks losing Hawk, the only man she has ever loved. Readers will find themselves quickly drawn into this fast-paced novel of treachery, intrigue, spiritual discovery, and unexpected love.

Everlasting, Amanda MacLean
ISBN 0-88070-929-4

Picking up where the captivating *Stonehaven* left off, *Everlasting* brings readers face to face once more with charming, courageous—and very Irish—Sheridan O'Brian. Will she find her missing twin? And will Marcus Jade, a reporter bent on finding out what really happened to Shamus, destroy his chances with her by being less than honest?

Betrayed, Lorena McCourtney
ISBN 0-88070-756-9

As part of a wealthy midwestern family, young Rosalyn Fallon was sheltered from the struggles brought on by the Depression. But when her father's company collapses and her boyfriend and best friend elope, Rosalyn unexpectedly finds herself facing both hardship and heartbreak. Will her new life out West and a man as rugged and rough as the land itself help her recover?

Escape, Lorena McCourtney
ISBN 1-57673-012-3

Is money really everything? The winsome Beth Curtis must come to terms with that question as she fights to hold on to guardianship of her nephew, even facing her deceased sister-in-law's brother. Sent to collect the boy, handsome Guy Wilkerson has no idea that he will fall for Beth, and come to see his own family's ways of living in a new light. Can the two overcome such diversity to be together, beginning their own family?

Voyage, Elaine Schulte
ISBN 1-57673-011-5
Traveling via cruise ship to the Holy Land, Ann Marie is on a pilgrimage, discovering things about faith and love all the way. But will a charming man who guides her—among the romantic streets of Greece and elsewhere—distract her from the One who truly loves her?

A Christmas Joy, MacLean, Darty, Gillenwater
ISBN 0-88070-780-1 (same length as other Palisades books)
Snow falls, hearts change, and love prevails! In this compilation, three experienced Palisades authors spin three separate novelettes centering around the Christmas season and message.
By Amanda MacLean: A Christmas pageant coordinator in a remote mountain village of Northern California is reunited with an old friend and discovers the greatest gift of all.
By Peggy Darty: A college ski club reunion brings together model Heather Grant and an old flame. Will they gain a new understanding?
By Sharon Gillenwater: A chance meeting in an airport that neither of them could forget...and a Christmas reunion.

Mistletoe: Ball, Hicks, McCourtney (October, 1996)
ISBN 1-57673-013-1
A new Christmas anthology of three novellas...all in one keepsake book!